MARK

WESLEY BIBLE STUDIES

wphonline.com

Copyright © 2014 by Wesleyan Publishing House
Published by Wesleyan Publishing House
Indianapolis, Indiana 46250
Printed in the United States of America
ISBN: 978-0-89827-838-5
ISBN (e-book): 978-0-89827-839-2

CONTENTS

INTRODUCTION

Where the Action Is

Modern culture loves action. It seems almost everything we watch, drive, wear, drink, eat, and do must promise or deliver some kind of action. Marketing gurus promise action-packed drama, action-filled entertainment, the latest in active sportswear, and equipment that promises a rewarding workout. "Just do it!" is a slogan readily identified with a brand of sportswear. Our love of action fills football stadiums and ice hockey arenas, where the price of a ticket, the cost to park, and refreshments can easily zap a fan's wallet to the tune of two hundred dollars—or more. Some action-loving football fans shell out thousands of dollars to attend a Super Bowl. What is especially frustrating during a game is to leave your seat to visit a concession stand, return several minutes later, only to hear a friend say, "You missed the action! Our team scored two touchdowns while you were gone."

It would be a shame to miss any part of the gospel of Mark, because it delivers action that impacts life and eternity. Mark's inspired narrative offers the good news of Jesus (Mark 1:1) to the whole world, but it was directed primarily toward the action-loving Romans. They could see Jesus in action and be attracted to Him.

CAMEOS OF JESUS IN ACTION

Unlike the gospel of Luke, Mark contains only a few parables, but its chapters are chock-full of cameos of Jesus in action. Early in the gospel, we find John the Baptist preparing Israel for its

Messiah, who suddenly comes to the Jordan River to be baptized by John. Our next view of Jesus shows Him calling four fishermen to follow Him. From that point—in the synagogue, in a house, in open fields—we read about Him healing, changing lives, feeding a multitude, silencing a raging storm, giving mobility to a paralyzed man, expelling demons, enabling a deaf mute to hear and speak, and granting sight to a blind man. We see the active Messiah take three disciples up a high mountain and give them a glimpse of His dazzling glory. Immediately (this word occurs often in the action-packed gospel of Mark) after leaving the mountain, we read about Jesus healing a demon-possessed boy.

CAMEOS OF JESUS' TRIUMPHAL ENTRY, DEATH, AND RESURRECTION

The action doesn't slow as we approach the end of Mark's gospel. We see Jesus setting a vigorous pace as He leads His disciples toward Jerusalem, where crowds welcome Him. He gathers His disciples together and paints graphic pictures of end-time events. Later, He engages in earnest prayer in Gethsemane. His subsequent arrest, betrayal, and crucifixion come at us in quick succession, but the agony of seeing Jesus mocked, beaten, and nailed to a cross fills our hearts with grief. We shed tears as we see Him die.

But Jesus triumphs over death. He voluntarily assumed an active role in the crucifixion by choosing to die for us, and He assumed an active role in defeating death by rising from the grave.

We serve a living Savior. He is actively interceding for us in heaven and actively empowering us for a life of holiness and service. May our study of Mark's gospel help us to be all He wants us to be!

JESUS IS THE GOOD NEWS

Mark 1:1–20

Jesus invites us to join Him in sharing this
transformational message.

Although greatly outnumbered by Persian soldiers on the plains of Marathon in Greece, the Athenian army defeated the Persians. The victorious army dispatched Phidippides, a runner, to carry the good news of the victory to Athens, twenty-six miles away. Phidippides covered the distance in about three hours and delivered the good news. He died shortly thereafter from exhaustion.

Good news about Jesus, who offers forgiveness and new life, is worth delivering, even if doing so carries a heavy personal cost. This study portrays John the Baptist as an exemplary messenger of this good news, and it motivates us to proclaim the good news as well.

COMMENTARY

The gospel of Mark reads like an eyewitness account of Jesus—the eyewitness long thought to be the apostle Peter. Many scholars think Mark's author, John Mark, served as the personal secretary of the apostle Peter, recording with precision the details of Jesus' life as remembered by the apostle. Thus, Mark is known as "Peter's gospel."

While Mark is the shortest of the Gospels, it is the most active, perhaps revealing the impulsive disposition of Peter. The word *immediately* appears over forty times. The book contains only one long teaching discourse (ch. 13) and four parables, but eighteen miracles are cited.

John Mark wrote during the time of Roman peace (*pax romana*) in the world, but simultaneously with the persecution of Nero, the Roman emperor. The content of the book, which often explains Jewish words and customs, indicates it was written to non-Jewish readers. Several Latin words are used, and the time of events is reported in Roman time. As our study progresses in Mark, notice the vivid eyewitness details of events and actions found in the book.

The Long-Expected Good News of Jesus Christ (Mark 1:1–8)

Mark spent little time laying the groundwork for the ministry actions of Jesus. While Matthew and Luke begin with genealogies, Mark's brief prologue points directly to **Jesus Christ, the Son of God** (v. 1)—the One whom the prophet John the Baptist declared as **more powerful than I . . . whose sandals I am not worthy to stoop down and untie** (v. 7).

John Mark emphasized that the arrival of Jesus was expected and broadly announced. The gospel or good news about Jesus Christ had been declared long ago by both Malachi (Mal. 3:1) and Isaiah the prophet (Isa. 40:3). Malachi was written in the fifth century B.C. and Isaiah in the eighth. Almost a thousand years later, John the Baptist announced the fulfillment of these prophecies.

Mark's prologue would have been easily understood by non-Jewish readers. It was typical for the Romans to send a herald ahead of prominent officials to announce their coming. Heralds often brought the good news of a royal birth, which indicated the beginning of a new age for the empire. John, the **messenger ahead of** Jesus, announced the coming of both the person of Jesus Christ and the kingdom He would initiate (Mark 1:2).

John prepared **the way** and made **straight paths** for the coming of the Son of God (vv. 2–3). Cyril of Jerusalem noted that John's message was the crown of the prophetic tradition and the firstfruits of the gospel. His preaching—**a baptism of repentance for the**

forgiveness of sins (v. 4)—signaled the core of the salvation message found in the person of Jesus Christ.

Water baptism was common in the first century for those who converted to Judaism, but John infused new meaning into the rite— baptism as a sign of **repentance for the forgiveness of sins** (v. 4). John required confession and repentance prior to baptism even for the children of Abraham. Repentance means not merely being sorry for sin, but literally hating it to the extent that the repentant turns away from a sinful life to a new life in Christ. John taught confession and repentance as necessary for forgiveness and genuine pardon.

The people of the **Judean countryside** responded to John's message and came to him for baptism (v. 5). Certainly John was not the draw, for he was clothed not in a business suit, but in the rough animal skin of **camel's hair** and wearing a **leather belt**. He was a mountain man of sorts whose diet consisted of **locusts and wild honey** (v. 6).

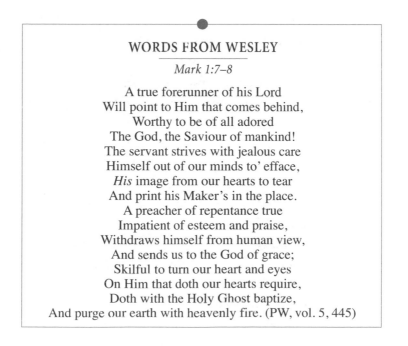

WORDS FROM WESLEY

Mark 1:7–8

A true forerunner of his Lord
Will point to Him that comes behind,
Worthy to be of all adored
The God, the Saviour of mankind!
The servant strives with jealous care
Himself out of our minds to' efface,
His image from our hearts to tear
And print his Maker's in the place.
A preacher of repentance true
Impatient of esteem and praise,
Withdraws himself from human view,
And sends us to the God of grace;
Skilful to turn our heart and eyes
On Him that doth our hearts require,
Doth with the Holy Ghost baptize,
And purge our earth with heavenly fire. (PW, vol. 5, 445)

But John's message was powerful and full of optimism. He announced the coming of the age of the long-expected kingdom of heaven with the Messiah who would bring salvation. This powerful man who would follow would not merely baptize **with water, but he will baptize you with the Holy Spirit** (v. 8). Indeed John's message was good news—better than any herald had previously announced.

The Good News of Jesus Christ Is Confirmed (Mark 1:9–13)

The good news of Jesus Christ is not without other witnesses. Its reality is confirmed not only by the prophecies of Isaiah and Malachi, but by the confirmation of God himself, and Satan, the enemy of all good.

John the Baptist must have been surprised the day **Jesus came from Nazareth** to be **baptized by John in the Jordan** (v. 9). Scripture records that John was apprehensive (see Matt. 3:13–15) but eventually consented. At the moment **Jesus was coming up out of the water**, the presence of God invaded history in a way never seen before or since (Mark 1:10). The heavens were **torn open** (something only the God of heaven could do), and Jesus saw **the Spirit descending on him like a dove. And a voice** said, **"You are my Son, whom I love; with you I am well pleased"** (vv. 10–11). This account not only confirms the deity of Jesus Christ as God's Son, but records the presence of the triune God.

The debate over Jesus Christ as God and human would command the attention of the church for its first three centuries. Those present at Jesus' baptism, while undoubtedly awestruck with amazement, were witnesses of the Trinity at work. All three entities of God were present—God the Father speaking from heaven, God the Holy Spirit appearing as a dove, and God the Son accepting the blessing of the heavenly Father. Notice here that God in three persons is recognizable; He is not merely changing from one personality to another. The triune God, present from before creation and continuing into the infinite future, in that moment of human history, was readily recognizable.

But the confirmation of Jesus as God's Son did not come solely from God. Satan himself weighed in on the matter. Scripture vividly records Jesus sent by the **Spirit . . . out into the desert**, where he was **tempted by Satan** for a period of **forty days** (vv. 12–13; see also Matt. 4; Luke 4). From these passages, we understand that Satan recognized the severe challenge the coming of Christ would be to his authority. Here, before Jesus even began His divinely appointed task, Satan worked to dissuade Jesus from His mission. This incident is more than symbolic, but demonstrates Satan as a real being, working to overthrow the authority of heaven. While his days of prominence are numbered (see Rev. 20), his present arts of deception are not to be taken lightly or ignored.

God's Son was not abandoned during those forty days in the desert, but **angels attended him** (Mark 1:13). Through reliance upon the strength of the heavenly Father, He was able to overcome temptation and refrain from falling into the Tempter's grasp. The human Jesus endured Satan's most heinous devices, yet overcame. In the same way, men and women today can overcome temptation through the strength of the same heavenly Father. Victory over temptation is not by our own power, but with the strength of God that lies within us (1 Cor. 10:13).

Temptation is not sin, but when we give in to it, it becomes sin. Gregory the Great, in the sixth century, wrote, "The dynamic of temptation proceeds first by suggestion, then by taking delight in the suggestion, then by consent." God through the Holy Spirit enables us to curb and dismiss the power of temptation at its early stages. Our delight in temptation only leads toward the sin that can entrap.

The good news of Jesus Christ as the Son of God, confirmed both by God and Satan, should cause us great encouragement when we face temptation. "Therefore, since we have a great high priest who has gone through the heavens, Jesus the Son of God, let us hold firmly to the faith we profess. For we do not have a high priest who is unable to sympathize with our weaknesses, but we have one who has been tempted in every way, just as we are—yet was without sin. Let us then approach the throne of grace with confidence, so that we may receive mercy and find grace to help us in our time of need" (Heb. 4:14–16).

The Good News of Jesus Christ Calls for Action (Mark 1:14–20)

Jesus knew the **time** had **come**. His message—**"The kingdom of God is near. Repent and believe the good news!"** (v. 15)— built upon and fulfilled the message (v. 4) the now-imprisoned John had preached (v. 14). The time indicated here is not a particular hour, but the opportune or seasonable time much like a parent would say to his or her child, "It is time you learned to drive." Jesus' message proclaimed not only repentance and belief in the good news, but the coming of the kingdom of God (v. 15).

●

WORDS FROM WESLEY

Mark 1:15

In the children of God, repentance and faith exactly answer each other. By repentance we feel the sin remaining in our hearts, and cleaving to our words and actions: By faith, we receive the power of God in Christ, purifying our hearts, and cleansing our hands. By repentance, we are still sensible that we deserve punishment for all our tempers, and words, and actions: By faith, we are conscious that our Advocate with the Father is continually pleading for us, and thereby continually turning aside all condemnation and punishment from us. By repentance we have an abiding conviction that there is no help in us: By faith, we receive not only mercy, "but grace to help in" *every* "time of need." Repentance disclaims the very possibility of any other help: Faith accepts all the help we stand in need of, from Him that hath all power in heaven and earth. Repentance says, "Without him I can do nothing:" Faith says, "I can do all things through Christ strengthening me." (WJW, vol. 5, 168)

To assist in the proclamation of the good news, Jesus began recruiting followers. He did not simply conscript persons with time on their hands, but busy people with energy and full-time occupations. Today's leader knows, "If you want something done, ask a busy person." Jesus himself used this strategy as He recruited His disciples.

As Jesus walked beside the Sea of Galilee (v. 16), He saw men plying their fishing trade, something one can still see along Galilee. Fishing was a major industry in Galilee. Josephus, a first-century governor of Galilee, recorded 330 fishing boats. These men were not fishing alone. One group was accompanied by **their father Zebedee** and **hired men** (v. 20). Yet Jesus seemed intent to pick certain ones from the groups of fishermen and called, **"I will make you fishers of men"** (v. 17). **At once** and **without delay** the fisherman left their work and **followed him** (vv. 18, 20). Why would one leave his livelihood and follow a stranger, unless he somehow knew the stranger offered a much fuller life?

WORDS FROM WESLEY

Mark 1:17–18

See that you "wait upon the Lord without distraction:" Let nothing move you from your centre. "One thing is needful;" to see, love, follow Christ, in every thought, word, and work. (WJW, vol. 14, 462)

Much could be said about Jesus' call to His early disciples. He must have spoken with authority, as He called for complete obedience. There was something divinely compelling about His call. It is reasonable to think that Simon, Andrew, James, and John had heard the message of Jesus, and perhaps even been baptized earlier by John the Baptist or Jesus himself. In following Jesus, these men would learn that discipleship is ultimate obedience to the Savior.

Our response to Christ's call is often riddled with excuses: It takes too much time; I can't commit; I'm enjoying life; and so on. Yet these disciples simply obeyed. "It is preposterous from the world's point of view that those without education could be used to instruct the nations" (Eusebius); yet through twelve obedient disciples, the good news of Jesus Christ has resulted in the salvation of millions of men, women, and children throughout the centuries.

Note the rapidity of movement present in the first twenty verses of Mark's gospel. The writing of John Mark moves us quickly into the story line of Jesus' ministry, demonstrates action speaking as loudly as words, and provides the further context for the action of the chapters that follow.

DISCUSSION

If you received good news that many people had been waiting to hear for a long time, wouldn't you share it enthusiastically? John the Baptist proclaimed the long-anticipated good news of Jesus unreservedly.

1. Why do you agree or disagree that it is significant that Mark's gospel is just "the beginning of the gospel about Jesus Christ" (Mark 1:1)?

2. What do you learn from John's example about genuine humility?

3. How did John's ministry prepare the way for Jesus? Do you think people today need to repent and be baptized in order to receive forgiveness? Why or why not? If you disagree, explain how people today can receive forgiveness.

4. Read Mark 1:9–11. Why do you think Jesus was baptized?

5. Do you agree or disagree that although Jesus was tempted He could not have sinned?

6. Compare Mark 1:12–13 and Matthew 4:1. What role did the Spirit play in Jesus' temptation? How do you explain this role?

7. According to Mark 1:16–20, four fishermen immediately answered Jesus' call to follow Him. What cost was involved in their decision? What might it cost believers today to follow Jesus? Is following Him worth the cost? Explain.

PRAYER

Lord, thank You for raising people like John the Baptist to prepare people's hearts to meet You. Give us the courage to step into that role as the Holy Spirit leads us today.

2

RENEWAL COMES THROUGH TIME WITH GOD

Mark 1:21–39

Time with God empowers our service.

When streetcars transported passengers up and down city streets, they ran quietly and efficiently unless their connecting rod became detached from the overhead power line. Until the conductor put the rod back in place, his streetcar stood motionless on the track and failed to fulfill its purpose.

This study discloses the vital power link between Jesus and His authoritative ministry. He spent time with His heavenly Father. Our power for service is directly related to the time we spend with God. Little prayer, little power. Much prayer, much power.

COMMENTARY

The message of good news had to somehow be widely communicated in the context of first-century Palestine. Unlike today when technology can instantly send news around the globe, such communication tools were unheard of in the first century.

Strategically speaking, the best place to communicate a religious message in the first century was in the synagogue. So, as was the normal custom, "when the Sabbath came, Jesus went into the synagogue" (Mark 1:21). Jesus' early visits to the synagogue set the tone for His authoritative ministry for the next three years.

Authority figures often seem bigger than life. They have earned or occupy a position of respect among others. Certainly such authority can be used for good or for ill. We may rightly question authority, endeavoring to discern its use or abuse based on the principles of God's Word.

But consider the person of Jesus. Mark 1 describes Jesus' hearers as recognizing Him as "one who had authority" (1:22). Where did His authority come from? Why did He possess it? To what would it lead? This chapter reveals answers to these questions as we see Jesus begin to demonstrate His authority over both earthly and spiritual realms.

Jesus Exercised Authority over Evil Spirits (Mark 1:21–28)

The synagogue was a place of teaching. Its services consisted of prayer, reading, and exposition of God's Word. Built to face Jerusalem, the synagogue served as a school during the week and on the Sabbath (Saturday) was the place Jewish men would gather to hear the reading and teaching of the Torah.

The ruler of the synagogue arranged for its weekly services. There was no teacher-in-residence, but this role was often filled by itinerants who traveled from synagogue to synagogue. Such persons were called upon regularly by the ruler to bring the teaching exposition.

Thus, it was not unusual for Jesus to attend service at the synagogue and to be called upon as an itinerant preacher to bring the morning exposition (v. 21). But Jesus' message was certainly different from the norm. Those who heard Him **were amazed** not just at *what* He taught, but *how* He taught (v. 22).

Rabbis did not typically speak on their own authority; rather they appealed to the authority of their predecessors or other experts in the law. Jesus, however, spoke with personal authority. He needed no external expert, but spoke with complete independence. He appealed to them as the final voice of God himself. The amazement of Jesus' hearers (vv. 22, 27) led to **news about him** that **spread quickly over the whole region of Galilee** (v. 28).

Jesus' message was unique for His good news taught the coming of the kingdom of God, repentance, and belief in the good news (1:15). But not only did Jesus' words captivate His audience, His deeds did as well. When confronted boldly by a man in the synagogue **who was possessed by an evil spirit** (v. 23), Jesus demonstrated His authority over the realm of evil spirits.

"What do you want with us, Jesus of Nazareth?" the demon asked. **"Have you come to destroy us? I know who you are—the Holy One of God!"** (v. 24). Here, in the presence of the religious men of the synagogue in Capernaum, the evil world itself identified Jesus as **the Holy One of God**. The kingdom of Satan gave way to the kingdom of God, recognizing the authority and credentials of Jesus Christ, God's Son.

WORDS FROM WESLEY

The Need for Healing

When man came first out of the hands of the great Creator, clothed in body as well as in soul with immortality and incorruption, there was no place for physic or the art of healing. As he knew no sin, so he knew no pain, no sickness, weakness, or bodily disorder. . . . But since man rebelled against the Sovereign of heaven and earth, how entirely is the scene changed! The incorruptible frame hath put on corruption, the immortal has put on mortality. The seeds of weakness and pain, of sickness and death, are now lodged in our inmost substance; whence a thousand disorders continually spring, even without the aid of external violence. (WJW, vol. 14, 307)

Unwilling to have one of His created beings be victimized by the evil spirit, Jesus sternly commanded the spirit to be muzzled as a farmer would muzzle an ox and said, **"Come out of him!"** (v. 25). Without an alternative to the direct and authoritative command of God's Son, **the evil spirit shook the man violently and came out of him with a shriek** (v. 26). His departure was not without a fight as he attempted one last time to cause the man to unnaturally convulse and shriek.

Exorcists were common in the first century and relied upon elaborate incantations and magic rites to exorcise demons from a person. Jesus' method of exorcism was decidedly different. He spoke with authority, and with a simple word commanded the demon to leave. The power of Jesus' action was not in His spell-binding words, but in His authoritative person.

This unusual act of the Sabbath-teaching rabbi, combined with the authoritative new message and way in which it was delivered, caused amazement among *all* the people who heard Jesus (v. 27). John Mark said that the **news about him spread quickly over the whole region of Galilee** (v. 28). Crowds began to seek out Jesus, recognizing His **new teaching . . . with authority**, and the authority He exercised over the **evil spirits** that obeyed Him (v. 27).

Jesus Exercised Authority over Disease (Mark 1:29–34)

As soon as they left the synagogue (notice again Mark's rapid movement description), Jesus—accompanied by **James, John**, Simon, and Andrew—went **to the home of Simon and Andrew** (v. 29). Simon and Andrew's home was to serve as the home base for Jesus' ministry while He was in the northern region of Galilee. Notice that Jesus was no longer alone in His ministry endeavors but now accompanied by four disciples.

Upon arriving at the home, Simon was probably confronted by his wife, who reported that her mother was **in bed with a fever** (v. 30). This was no minor concern in the age before antibiotics. Jesus, upon hearing this report, immediately and directly responded to her need. **He went to her, took her hand and helped her up. The fever left her and she began to** attend to the needs of her guests (v. 31). This incident likely remained clearly etched in Peter's mind as he reported it to John Mark for recording in this gospel. He remembered the incident and the care and concern with which Jesus touched his mother-in-law.

Word that Jesus was in Capernaum spread. Perhaps it was news of His healings in the region or that He had touched the mother-in-law of Simon. In any case, **the whole town gathered at the door** of Simon's home (v. 33). Notice again John Mark's attention to detail. This may or may not have literally been the whole town, but the intent is the same as if we would say, "Everyone was in church Sunday." This was no small crowd, but the majority of those who resided in the area of Capernaum.

As respectful Jews, they had waited until **that evening after sunset** (v. 32). The Jewish Sabbath extended from sunset Friday to sunset Saturday. During that time it was unlawful to bear burdens and violate the Sabbath (Jer. 17:21–22). The Sabbath ended according to Jewish Law when three stars came out in the sky.

Jesus was responsive to the plight of the people and **healed many who had various diseases. He also drove out many demons** (v. 34). Jesus' empathy for afflicted people and His authority over demons and disease continued to be exhibited, not on one or two occasions, but time after time.

WORDS FROM WESLEY

Jesus' Power to Heal

Help, gracious Lord, my deep distress
To Thee with anguish I reveal,
Who every sickness and disease
Dost still among Thy people heal. (WJW, vol. 5, 376)

But he would not let the demons speak because they knew who he was (v. 34). This appears to be a puzzling statement. Why would the Holy One of God, as recognized by the demons and others who had been healed, prohibit them from declaring who He really was? This admonition of restraint is noted numerous times in the Gospels (see, for example, Mark 1:44; 3:12; 5:43; 7:36; 8:26).

WORDS FROM WESLEY

Mark 2:27

Christ would neither suffer those evil spirits to speak in opposition, nor yet in favour of Him. He needed not their testimony, nor would encourage it, lest any should infer, that He acted in concert with them. (ENNT)

Several possible explanations should be considered. First, in the case of demons, Jesus may not have wanted the demonic world to be witness to His presence. Such would be similar to a thief or a liar vouching for the credibility of a witness in a trial. Second, one must be attentive to the timing of Jesus' ministry. The fulfillment of prophecy had occurred after the patient waiting of people for hundreds of years. Hastening the incidents in the present moment would be premature. Third, much of the present interest in Jesus' ministry was due to His actions, His deeds of healing and exorcism. Jesus did not want His message of good news to be overshadowed by His healing ministry. Fourth, Jesus' mission was not yet clear to His followers. He did not desire to set up an earthly kingdom, but to be a Suffering Servant who would demonstrate victory over Satan's kingdom through His death and resurrection.

Three times in these verses Jesus healed people: in the synagogue, in the house of friends, and on the street outside Simon's home. Jesus recognized the needs of all persons and responded accordingly, whether they were presumed religious persons in the synagogue on the Sabbath, friends of the family, or people who seemingly had no connection whatsoever with religious circles.

Jesus' Authority Was Empowered by Time Alone with God (Mark 1:35–39)

Often we easily dismiss the actions of Jesus and are simply content to say, "Well, of course. He *was* God, after all!" We fail to grasp the extent of His humanness and the frailty of His physical being. Jesus' physical needs were just as real as ours are today. The rejuvenating of His physical body through sleep was absolutely necessary. Yet He also recognized that His spiritual being needed intentional rejuvenation as well.

Very early in the morning, while it was still dark, Jesus got up, left the house and went off to a solitary place, where he prayed (v. 35). Certainly Jesus must have been tired after the busyness of the previous day. The ministry pressures were still present, and ministry opportunities were numerous. But He left those behind to spend time in prayer with His Father early the next morning, probably during the first watch (between 3:00 and 6:00 a.m.) and in the dark. Jesus recognized the absolute necessity of time alone with God.

Scripture does not record whether He needed this time, but we can suspect that He *wanted* this time. If Jesus himself found it desirable and necessary to spend time alone with God His Father, how much more should we? Times of prayer, spiritual retreat, and meditation on things of God provide refreshment and food for the soul of the Christian.

After a time, **Simon and his companions went to look for** Jesus (v. 36). After finding him, **they exclaimed: "Everyone is looking for you!"** (v. 37). While Jesus seems not to have particularly enjoyed the attention He was receiving, His disciples almost gloried in it, or at least they let Jesus know that His presence was critical to accommodating the desires of the crowds.

Jesus' reply likely took them by surprise. Rather than return to the press of the crowds that were reveling in Jesus' presence, Jesus said, **"Let us go somewhere else** where the crowds have not yet gathered, and the pressures of ministry deeds have not yet been recognized. **I have come** so that **I can preach** in other villages also" (v. 38). Jesus knew His mission was not about performing for a crowd but about announcing the kingdom of God and repentance. The message must not be subsumed by the miracles.

The nearby villages in this passage would be those beyond Capernaum and **throughout Galilee.** And it was to these further villages that He traveled, **preaching in their synagogues and driving out demons** (v. 39). The spread of Jesus' message through the synagogues was being received, and the forces of the kingdom of darkness were being driven back as He cast out demons.

The crowds were enamored with Jesus' miracles and the authoritative message He proclaimed. But such came with a significant price, one that compelled the "Holy One of God" (1:24) to seek solitude and refreshment in prayer with the heavenly Father. The complete mission, focusing upon the cross, was yet to be announced, and soon the enthusiasm of the crowd would change.

DISCUSSION

Very early in life we learn that parents are authority figures. As we grow older, we accept additional authority figures: teachers, law enforcement officers, employers, and government officials, to name a few. But Jesus is our ultimate authority figure.

1. Why were the people in the synagogue amazed at Jesus' teaching? What do you find so amazing about His teaching?

2. How did the evil spirit acknowledge Jesus' authority?

3. How is it possible to recognize Jesus' authority without submitting to it? Why do you agree or disagree that there is a vast difference between an intellectual knowledge of Jesus and a heart knowledge of Him?

4. What perception of Jesus do you think the people of Galilee acquired (Mark 1:28)? What do you think is the most widespread perception of Jesus today? If you believe this perception is false, how might you help correct it?

5. What characteristics of Jesus do you find in Mark 1:29–34? How does an awareness of these characteristics encourage you?

6. Do you think it is possible to experience God's power in your life if you do not spend much time with Him? Explain.

7. Mark 1:38 discloses one of Jesus' main missions in life. What is God's main mission for your life? What are a few other missions God wants you to perform?

PRAYER

Lord, increase our confidence in Your power over disease and over those that exist in the realms of darkness. Ease our fears when we encounter forces that seem overwhelming. Remind us that Satan can do nothing without Your permission.

3

NO NEED BEYOND HIS REACH

Mark 2:1–17

Jesus meets our greatest needs.

A TV reporter asked a survivor of the July 20, 2012, movie massacre in Aurora, Colorado, how he managed to stay so calm. The survivor, a man in his early thirties, responded, "My faith is in Jesus."

As that survivor knew, Jesus is the Good Shepherd, who never abandons His sheep. He sympathizes with us in all our adversities, and He meets every need we have. He gives us peace on the operating table as well as at the dinner table.

Although many oppose Him, Jesus meets the need of salvation for everyone who believes in Him. This study demonstrates the fact that no need lies beyond His reach.

COMMENTARY

Miracles are events that produce astonishment and wonder, causing the Christian to marvel and sense an awareness of God. Some miracles may be spectacular, surpassing the bounds of human reason. Others may be found in ordinary events that transpire in such a way that God's hand is evident.

Mark 2 explores the extent of miracles. Events that seem insignificant at first may indeed be the greatest of God's miracles in our lives. In Mark 2, Jesus demonstrated His authority coupled with compassion in meeting the greatest need of an ordinary man. The man's presenting problem was displaced by Jesus touching a much deeper need.

Jesus Healed the Body and the Heart (Mark 2:1–5, 11–12)

Mark's portrayal of the paralytic is a more vivid account than what is found in either Matthew (9:1–8) or Luke (5:17–26). John Mark was the only one who named Capernaum (Mark 2:1), the only one who described the fullness of the room and the crowd outside the door (v. 2). John Mark was the only one who indicated the paralytic was carried by four men (v. 3). These are details that would have been added by an eyewitness such as Peter.

Jesus again entered Capernaum, and the people heard that he had come home (v. 1). **Home** here refers to Jesus' home base while teaching in the Galilee region. When word spread, the crowd grew so large **that there was no room left, not even outside the door** (v. 2). This may have been the same group of people from Capernaum that was noted in 1:33. The size of the crowd gathered around the home to hear Jesus preach **the word to them** must have been impressive. But through this mass of people, four men pressed toward Jesus. After an aborted attempt to walk through the crowd, they redirected their efforts toward the roof (2:4).

Approaching the rooftop would not have been difficult, once the men got through the crowd. Generally an outside stairway led to the roof, which was made of clay tiles reinforced with twigs and dirt. John Mark described the men as **digging through** the tiles, likely reminding Simon of the repair work he had to complete. These men **lowered the mat**—the word *mat* here is a Latin word in the original (something similar to a camp cot)— through the **opening in the roof** they had created (v. 4).

Jesus recognized these four as being full of faith, and their faith was rewarded when Jesus **said to the paralytic, "Son, your sins are forgiven"** (v. 5). One wonders how this action squared with the desired intentions of the four men. Did they expect Jesus to utter these words or to address what at least appeared to be more important—the physical healing of the man bound to the mat? Had these four considered the larger issue of the man's spiritual well-being?

It was commonly held among the Jews that sickness was a result of sin (John 9). Today, we recognize that sickness is not the direct result of an individual's sin (though it might be the logical consequences of sinful practice). Sickness is the result of life in a fallen world that groans under the curse of sin. We must be careful when we are confronted with physical ailments not to immediately associate them with sin. Such was the error of the religious leaders in John 9.

But here, Jesus recognized the man's greatest need was not his physical ailment, but the disease of his heart—his need for forgiveness of sins (Mark 2:5). Jesus addressed his spiritual need and unequivocally demonstrated His authority to forgive sins.

But in this incident, Jesus did not stop with forgiving the man's sins. He reached out further to the needs of the man and touched his physical condition as well, saying, **"Get up, take your mat and go home"** (v. 11). The paralytic obeyed without hesitation, and **walked out in full view of them all** (v. 12). John Mark's description enables one to easily imagine the man reaching down, gathering his makeshift bed, and walking merrily toward the door. The incident did not happen in a back room, but in the complete and open presence of all who were present.

John Mark again recorded the amazement of the crowd, who broke out in praise to God for this miracle. The extent of the healing, the wholeness of spiritual heart and physical body that Jesus gave to this man, was more than ample cause for rejoicing in the work of God (v. 12).

Jesus Met Opposition (Mark 2:6–10)

But there were those who were not satisfied. Those in the religious establishment were raising questions and denying the witness of others that this was indeed the Son of God. Notice how these verses contrast with the popularity Jesus experienced with the crowds in Mark 1. While the crowds followed, the religious leaders rejected Him and His message of forgiveness.

The **teachers of the law**—that is, those who were experts and knew the Torah and the prophecies of the Messiah as well—began to dialogue among themselves (v. 6). **"Why does this fellow talk like that? He's blaspheming! Who can forgive sins but God alone?"** (v. 7). The experts knew that only God can forgive sins, and only the priest could pronounce a person clean. These teachers of the law were protectors of the law, both written and verbal. Their jurisdiction was to determine adherence to that law and identify lawbreakers. The penalty for blaspheming was death (see Lev. 24:15), and it appeared that **this fellow** was guilty (Mark 2:7).

WORDS FROM WESLEY

Mark 2:6

But certain of the scribes—See whence the first offence cometh! As yet not one of the plain unlettered people were offended. They all rejoiced in the light, till these *men* of *learning* came, to put darkness for light; and light for darkness. We to all such blind guides! Good had it been for these if they had never been born. O God, let me never offend one of thy simple ones! Sooner let my tongue cleave to the roof of my mouth! (ENNT)

Jesus' act of forgiving sins should have distinctly identified Him to the teachers of the law as the fulfillment of prophecy as the One who would come with authority, power, and everlasting dominion, and whose kingdom will never be destroyed (see Dan. 7:13–14). And to further bring home His point, Jesus **knew . . . what they were thinking** and demonstrated His authority by responding to the undisclosed secrets of their thoughts (v. 8). God alone could do that.

To further show His **authority on earth to forgive sins** (v. 10), something that would be difficult to prove or disprove objectively, Jesus proceeded with a visible miracle. Jesus commanded the paralytic man to get up and go home (v. 11). Surely this outward miracle would help to demonstrate the validity of the inward miracle of forgiveness of sins. Both miracles demonstrated Jesus' authority—one over the spiritual realm and the other over His created realm.

The word correctly translated as **authority** (v. 10) in the NIV does not mean power. Jesus did not simply have more power than sin; He had complete authority over sin. Jesus did not at this point identify himself as God but as the **Son of Man** (v. 10). Here Jesus, as the Son of Man, was claiming the prophetic right to speak for God. His actions were His own. He did not need to call upon His heavenly Father for assistance.

The Calling of Levi (Mark 2:13–14)

Verse 13 begins another story in Jesus' life. Probably because of the continued press of a **large crowd**, Jesus once again **went out beside the lake** (v. 13). Not only does the lake area provide sufficient space for such large gatherings, but also along the Sea of Galilee near Capernaum there are a number of rolling hills that would allow for the natural amplification of one's voice, as well as provide excellent seating so all could see. While He was walking along and teaching, Jesus **saw Levi son of Alphaeus sitting at the tax collector's booth. "Follow me," Jesus told him, and Levi got up and followed** (v. 14). This same Levi, or Matthew, would later write the first gospel.

Jesus' call to Levi was brief. The Gospels do not record a lengthy conversation, but rather a brief invitation and an immediate response. Levi's response was similar to the four fishermen whom Jesus had called in Mark 1; however, Levi left *all* to follow Jesus. The fishermen could readily return to their tasks of fishing, but Levi would not be able to return to his work. His tax booth, possibly taxing the fishing industry itself, would have been quickly occupied by another. Yet Levi followed Jesus into an entirely new way of life.

Jesus Met More Opposition (Mark 2:15–16)

A second occasion for opposition arose **while Jesus was having dinner at Levi's house** (v. 15), His most recently called disciple. Levi had gathered **many tax collectors and "sinners"** at his home for a feast (v. 15). These were likely acquaintances of Levi from his life as a tax collector, and persons despised by others because of their occupation.

WORDS FROM WESLEY

Mark 2:15

Many publicans and notorious *sinners sat with Jesus*—Some of them doubtless invited by Matthew, moved with compassion for his old companions in sin. But the next words, *For they were many, and they followed him*, seem to imply, that the greater part, encouraged by his gracious words and the tenderness of his behaviour, and impatient to hear more, staid [waited] for no invitation, but pressed in after him, and kept as close to him as they could. (ENNT)

Tax collectors were hated because they represented the occupying Roman force, and they unscrupulously excised more tax than was due and pocketed the difference. They were cheaters and corrupt to the extent that they were prohibited from holding public office or serving as witnesses in court. Money from tax collectors was considered so filthy that it was not even accepted for the poor at the temple.

Sinners in this text represented Jews who ignored the Mosaic law in both the ritual and moral sense. They were seen as irreligious and unobservant of the traditions of the elders. These two groups of people, while likely affluent, were looked down on by the teachers of the law.

So the religious establishment found two reasons in this gathering to oppose the ministry of Jesus. First, He seemed to blaspheme, assuming the role of God in forgiving sins. Second, He associated with **tax collectors** and **sinners**, persons known to be vile and without religious scruples (v. 16).

But the heart of the rejection and opposition by the teachers of the law was not the *practices* of Jesus, but their refusal to accept His *authority* on earth and by implication in the spiritual realm, the authority to forgive sins. They were faced with a need to respond to the question: Is this Jesus the prophesied Messiah?

Jesus Affirmed His Mission (Mark 2:17)

In the context of the demonstration of His authority, and despite the growing opposition of the teachers of the law, Jesus was clearly aware of His mission. His response to the teachers of the law was succinct and no doubt pierced to the heart of their motives (v. 17).

The teachers of the law were faced with the reality of the person of Jesus Christ and His claims: "I have authority as the Creator over both the spiritual and the physical realms. Will you acknowledge this and submit to My authority? I have not come to challenge those who are truly righteous but to aid the sinner." Clearly, Jesus knew His purpose.

WORDS FROM WESLEY

Mark 2:17

I came not to call the righteous— Therefore if these were righteous, I should not call them. But now, they are the very persons I came to save. (ENNT)

Why would a doctor visit the healthy? Would a doctor not visit the sick (v. 17)? In so doing, the doctor encounters and must deal with the pain of the sick, the emotional stresses of disease, and the stench of decay. But the person and role of the doctor brings healing in the middle of these terrors.

Jesus in the same way desires to encounter the pain and sickness of the sinner in order to bring spiritual healing. His mission is clear: to help those who carry the pain of sin and to bring forgiveness.

Jesus clearly knew His authority was over both the physical and spiritual realms. He was Lord of both heaven and earth. And in so being, His healing was completely sufficient for the needy in both realms. No matter how difficult the criticism, the Christian must remember that the good news of Jesus Christ comes with authority to heal the sickness of both the body and the heart.

DISCUSSION

Martin Luther said, "Man only needs Jesus Christ." He was right. Jesus saves, strengthens, sustains, and befriends us forever. However, many people reject Jesus and His willingness to meet every need.

1. Based on your reading of Mark 2:1–5, what would you identify as Jesus' highest priority?

2. How would you respond if someone claimed Christians should be more concerned about alleviating hunger, pain, and poverty than about sharing the message of salvation?

3. Why did Jesus' presence in the Capernaum house attract such a large crowd? What do you think it takes to draw a large crowd to church today?

4. What do you find commendable about the men who lowered the paralyzed man through the roof to Jesus?

5. What actions might you and/or your fellow Christians take to introduce some friends to Jesus?

6. What evidences do you see that indicate we live in a fallen world?

7. Why do you think the religious establishment opposed Jesus? Why might a religious leader today oppose Jesus?

8. How does it encourage you to know Jesus successfully called a tax collector to follow Him?

9. Why do you agree or disagree that Christians should be cautious about socializing with unbelievers?

PRAYER

Lord, let us never discriminate when it comes to serving people and sharing the gospel. If there are any prejudices within us, give us the courage to acknowledge them and root them out.

GOD'S WORD PROVIDES A HARVEST

Mark 4:10–20, 26–34

The seed of God's Word, when it is sown, produces a harvest.

An elderly man's hearing was poor, and at the request of concerned family members he visited an audiologist. After examining her patient, the audiologist fitted him with a pair of invisible hearing aids. Two weeks later, when the patient returned for a follow-up visit, the audiologist asked if he was pleased with the results. "Oh, yes," he replied. "I can hear clearly now."

"I'm glad to hear that," the audiologist replied. "Your family members must be pleased, too."

The patient winked. "I haven't told them yet. And guess what? I've changed my will three times since getting my hearing aids." In this study, we will learn that Jesus explained that how we hear God's Word determines how we act.

COMMENTARY

In Mark 4, we see a shift in Jesus' ministry. His popularity among the people was increasingly raising suspicion among the religious authorities. So Jesus departed from regular teaching in the synagogue and moved to teaching in the open along the lakeside, where the crowds of ordinary men and women would have greater opportunity to hear His message.

Jesus' departure to open-air preaching must have struck many in the traditional religious community as stunning and sensational, but He was wise enough to know when new methods were necessary and adventurous enough to use them.

Jesus' illustration of the farmer sowing seed would have been well understood in His day. He may have turned from His floating pulpit in the boat and said, "Look over there on the hill. There is a farmer sowing seed . . ." as He began to tell the story. The farmer followed standard practice—carrying seed in a knapsack along his side, reaching in for handful after handful, and throwing it gently to the wind to distribute it along the row. As he walked along scattering the seed gently into the wind, the seed fell onto four different kinds of soil.

The Secret of the Kingdom of God (Mark 4:10–13)

When the crowds disappeared and Jesus **was alone, the Twelve and the others around him asked him about the parables** (v. 10). Particular attention must be given to Jesus' explanation, as this is the sole parable explained by Jesus in the Gospels. Plus, Jesus indicated that this one in particular must be understood if we are to **understand any parable** (v. 13).

Verses 11–12 seem particularly confusing. Did Jesus really mean that He taught in parables so that the inner circle of disciples could understand and those outside the kingdom might never understand? In other words, was Jesus saying, "I'm trying to be confusing so others will not be forgiven" (vv. 11–12)?

Remember the broader context. In Mark 1, John the Baptist heralded the arrival of the promised Messiah, Jesus the Christ, whom he later baptized and who was affirmed at that baptism by both God the Father and the Holy Spirit. Jesus then began His ministry preaching in the conventional place, the synagogue, and healing and was increasingly criticized by the religious leaders. The criticism was so great that the teachers of the law accused Him of being possessed by the prince of demons himself (3:22)!

Now the reception of Jesus' message had changed. It was not being received by the religious leaders, and the crowds in general seemed to be wanting His healing power more than His message.

Jesus' intent of using parables was not to place forgiveness beyond the reach of those who genuinely seek it, but to point the listeners to the **secret of the kingdom of God** (4:11). The secret John the Baptist had already announced was the person of Christ himself. Jesus declared the kingdom is now here, but were the crowds listening? If one continually sees but never perceives or hears but never understands, forgiveness will not be present. One must take the message that is seen and heard, respond to it, and put it into action (v. 12).

WORDS FROM WESLEY

Mark 4:11–12

11. *To them that are without*—So the Jews termed the heathens: so our Lord terns all obstinate unbelievers: for they shall not enter into His kingdom: they shall abide in outer darkness.

12. *So that seeing they see and do not perceive*—They would not see before: now they could not, God having given them up to the blindness which they had chosen. (ENNT)

Consider an illustration from the classroom. What happens when the teacher repeats the same truth over and over, but students simply sit there and refuse to pay attention? Is the problem that they don't understand because the teacher speaks in riddles or that they don't understand because they refuse to listen?

How disappointed Jesus must have been when His audience failed to listen to what He was actually saying! Their failure to try to wrestle with the truth of the kingdom and to understand it only demonstrated their stubborn resistance and continued ignorance of His message. As long as they resisted, the good news of Jesus Christ would not be within their grasp of understanding. Those willing to understand would do so; those unwilling would miss the truth entirely (v. 12).

Jesus noted that understanding this parable is crucial to the understanding of parables period. This parable was a key, perhaps not in its content, but in His efforts to use it to illustrate carefully the secrets of the kingdom of God (v. 13).

The Planted Seed Will Grow (Mark 4:14–20)

The explanation of this parable according to Jesus is quite clear. **The farmer sows the word** (v. 14). The word, or the seed, is the good news of Jesus Christ that John had already preached about. The farmer scatters seed indiscriminately on the ground, exercising no bias in where he thinks it may grow. Only later does the farmer know the results of his labor.

The farmer's seed falls on four types of soil, each of which produces some sort of yield. Regardless of what else the farmer does, something happens to the seed—it grows according to the type of soil it falls upon.

First, **some people are like seed along the path** (v. 15). Inevitably, some seed falls on the hard-packed paths that wind across the countryside. These paths are made by countless travelers' feet, which produce a concrete-like soil pavement, impenetrable to falling seed. Just as the birds following the farmer eat it up, Satan immediately comes along and steals the hearing of the Word from these recipients. Perhaps their lives are hardened by continual practice of sin or the continual rejection of ignoring the Word of God that they hear, and they have become indifferent to the Word. These people think that the Word is irrelevant to life and that they can get on well enough without it. Any good farmer knows that the hard soil must first be broken up and tilled before it can receive the seed.

A second group of people are **like seed sown on rocky places** (v. 16). Palestine is full of limestone rock scattered throughout the fields. Many of these rocks lie just below the soil line and are covered to the eye. These people **hear the word and at once receive it with joy** (v. 16), but though the limestone holds heat and moisture, in this shallow soil there is little opportunity to sink deep roots. The joyful reception of the good news soon dries up and withers away when troubles and persecution come (v. 17).

A third group of people **hear the word; but the worries of this life, the deceitfulness of wealth and the desires for other things come in and choke the word, making it unfruitful** (vv. 18–19). These are seeds that fall among thorns or briars. Thorns rob the nutrition and moisture from the soil and overtake weaker plants. Often, their root systems are well-established and difficult to eradicate.

These thorns generally come from two places: seed or roots that were not dug out completely in an earlier season. The farmer can cut off the top of the fibrous rooted weeds—even burn off the top so the field looks clean—but below the surface the roots are still there, and in due time the weeds revive in all their strength. How easy it is to be choked by the worries of life. Money, things, all of which can be good in themselves, can quickly replace God in our schedule or trusting God to take care of our needs (vv. 18–19).

WORDS FROM WESLEY
Mark 4:19

The desire of other things choke the word—a deep and important truth! The desire of any thing, otherwise than as it leads to happiness in God, directly tends to barrenness of soul. *Entering in*—Where they were not before. Let him therefore who has received and retained the word, see that no other desire then enter in, such as perhaps till then he never knew. (ENNT)

A fourth group of people **hear the word, accept it, and produce a crop** (v. 20) of varying amounts. These final seeds fall on good soil, and in turn a crop is produced, multiplying the seed **thirty,**

sixty or even a hundred times (v. 20). The rich, fertile, volcanic-based soil of Palestine was well-known for its famous crops, and high yields were not unusual.

Notice that all those who hear and accept produce a crop; and there is no indication that we must all produce one hundred times what was sown. Each hearer produces immense quantities. If one would say, "Everyone who brings me an apple, I will give you twenty in return," that would be a good crop! But such production comes only after listening carefully, taking the truth to heart, and committing oneself to what God will do with the seed within.

The Growing Seed (Mark 4:26–29)

The parable of the growing seed in verses 26–29 is clear as well. The same farmer widely **scatters seed on the ground** (v. 26). He is not carefully ensuring where each seed falls, but regardless of his further actions, **night and day, whether he sleeps or gets up, the seed sprouts and grows** (v. 27). The growth of the seed is a mystery to him. There is nothing he has done in particular to ensure this growth. He has only gone about his daily business—yet growth has occurred **though he does not know how** (v. 27).

All by itself is a phrase used only in verse 28 and again in Acts 12:10. In Acts, it occurs at the occasion of the opening of the prison gate allowing for Peter's escape. This is the same word from which we get our English word *automation*. John Mark's point is that the growth of the **kingdom of God** (v. 26) is beyond human understanding. It literally is automatic.

But the process takes time; it is not instantaneous. Over the course of weeks, the stalk, the head, the full kernel come about mysteriously but dependably. The speed of the seed's growth is not controlled by the one who scatters it. Such is a mystery beyond his imagination. But the man sows in the confidence that the grain will ripen and **the harvest** will **come** (v. 29).

WORDS FROM WESLEY

Mark 4:26

So is the kingdom of God—The inward kingdom is like seed *which a man casts into the ground*—This a preacher of the gospel casts into the heart. And he *sleeps and rises night and day*—That is, he has it continually in his thoughts. Mean time *it springs and grows up he knows not how*—Even he that sowed it cannot explain how it grows. For as the earth by a curious kind of mechanism, which the greatest philosophers cannot comprehend, does as it were spontaneously bring forth first the blade, then the ear, then the full corn in the ear: So the soul, in an inexplicable manner, brings forth, first weak graces, then stronger, then full holiness: and all this of itself, as a machine, whose spring of motion is within itself. Yet observe the amazing exactness of the comparison. The earth brings forth no corn (as the soul no holiness) without both the care and toil of man, and the benign influence of heaven. (ENNT)

The Mustard Seed (Mark 4:30–34)

The growth of the kingdom of God is further described in the parable of the mustard seed. The mustard seed, recognized in the ancient world as the smallest seed, is powerful though it is extremely small. "Small as a mustard seed" was a Jewish proverb to indicate a minute particle (v. 31). Yet when this smallest seed is planted, it **becomes the largest of all garden plants** with a height of ten to twelve feet, readily providing **big branches** for **birds** to **shade** themselves (v. 32).

Jesus' message centered upon the revelation of the kingdom of God. The secrets, or mysteries, of kingdom truths were revealed in the person of Jesus Christ and His teaching. On occasions when Jesus was alone with His disciples, this was the message He carefully explained to them and wanted them to understand. Jesus was revealing the hidden truths of the kingdom of God at the divinely appointed time. Now the time of the kingdom had come, and its revealing was to take place.

John Mark made it clear that parables were becoming a regular way Jesus spoke, even if only a selection of those parables are included in his book. **Jesus spoke the word** to the crowds **as much as they could understand** (v. 33). And **when he was alone with his own disciples, he explained everything** (v. 34). Jesus was about setting free, explaining, and interpreting the secrets of the kingdom of God to His disciples. We read those same words today.

DISCUSSION

Farmers plant seed with hopeful anticipation of a bountiful crop, but they know a successful harvest depends on what happens to the seed after it has been planted. Jesus described what might happen when the Word is sown.

1. What kinds of responses to the Word do you find in Mark 4:10–20?

2. Why do you agree or disagree that some hearers refuse to accept the message of God's Word because they don't want to adjust their preconceived notions about the Word?

3. How can a believer improve the way he or she listens to God's Word?

4. How does an emotional response to the Word differ from a response that genuinely affects our emotions?

5. Compare Isaiah 55:10–11 and Mark 4:20. How do these passages bolster your confidence in the power of God's Word?

6. How can a believer avoid becoming indifferent to the Word? How can a believer avoid falling victim to the deceitfulness of riches?

7. How does the growth of a mustard seed resemble the kingdom of God?

8. How might your church sow the seed of God's Word efficiently and extensively?

PRAYER

Lord, please keep our hearts cultivated and ready to receive Your Word, bearing fruit for the kingdom as You determine. Keep us aware of the Spirit's work in our lives, and give us wisdom not to resist Him.

5

TRUSTING IN THE MIDST OF TRIALS

Mark 4:35—5:8, 15–20

Trust in the Lord in every phase of life.

Whitewater rafting is popular in the western United States, but to a casual observer it appears to be an extremely risky way to spend a day. A raft can strike rocks, get caught in an eddy, or even flip over. However, most rafters who shoot the rapids claim every ride is exhilarating and safe as long as passengers follow their guide's instructions and realize he or she is with them from the journey's start to its end.

Life's journey presents many hazards and rough spots. It does not offer an uninterrupted smooth ride. Even believers encounter trials and unpleasant bumps along the way, but Jesus is our guide. If we follow His instructions and keep our eyes on Him, He will not fail us. This study stresses the importance of trusting Jesus in the midst of trials.

COMMENTARY

An evening trip across the Sea of Galilee (Mark 4:35) to escape the crowds should have posed no difficulty for the group of experienced fishermen who accompanied Jesus. They were familiar with the Sea of Galilee and had sailed in it often in plying their trade. They would have also been familiar with the sudden squalls that come from the eastern mountains, making the water quickly treacherous.

The Sea of Galilee is about thirteen miles long and eight miles wide and lies 680 feet below sea level. Because of the sudden storms that come upon the lake, most fishing is done early in the morning. As the air temperature rises during the day, afternoon storms often accompany the change in pressure, and when they occur at night, they are especially dangerous. But when Jesus tells you to cross the Sea at night, you trust Him to get you to your destination.

Jesus Demonstrated Authority over Nature (Mark 4:35–41)

When evening came the disciples set out with Jesus toward the more desolate eastern side of the Sea of Galilee (v. 35). Jesus evidently hoped to escape the crowds that no doubt had tired Him throughout the day. **Other boats** accompanied the boat Jesus and the disciples were in (v. 36).

John Mark then described how **a furious squall came up, and the waves broke over the boat, so that it was nearly swamped** (v. 37). Assuming John Mark received his information from the fisherman Peter, this must have been a significant storm for an experienced sailor to describe it as such.

Yet despite the formidable storm, Jesus laid sound asleep **in the stern** of the boat **on a cushion**—the guest seat in the fishing boat (v. 38). The disciples, probably disgusted that Jesus was sleeping while their lives were in danger, **woke him and said to him, "Teacher, don't you care if we drown?"** (v. 38).

Seemingly ignoring the attitude of His disciples, Jesus issued a simple command to the wind and the waves: **"Quiet! Be still!"** (v. 39). Jesus spoke to the natural elements as if they were a person who would respond accordingly. Immediately, **the wind died down and it was completely calm** (v. 39).

One would expect the response of the disciples to be joy and thankfulness, but they were still **afraid** and had **no faith** (v. 40). First they were afraid of the storm, and then they were **terrified** of the calm (v. 41). The word translated *terrified* indicates a cowardly fear. Why did their fear increase? Was this a legitimate response?

WORDS FROM WESLEY

Mark 4:40

Ask we, now the storm is laid,
Wherefore was my heart afraid?
Lord, with shame the cause I see,
Want of confidence in Thee.
But Thy love doth not despise
Nature's most imperfect cries,
Souls o'erwhelm'd with doubts and fears,
Faith which next to none appears.
Thou my little faith increase
Till my last temptations cease,
Till Thy goodness I adore
Safe on the eternal shore. (PW, vol. 10, 480–481)

The disciples were shocked that **even the wind and the waves obey him** (v. 41). The Teacher who had cast out demons, healed the sick, and forgiven sins in the name of God now exercised unequivocal authority over the elements of nature. He who was master and creator of the winds and water commanded their obedience by His spoken word.

This was the first of many rebukes of His disciples (v. 40; compare 7:18; 8:17, 21, 32; 9:19). Jesus' disciples did not yet have enough faith to perceive the kingdom presence of Jesus. Jesus spent private time with the disciples, explaining to them the secrets of the kingdom of God (4:11), yet when they were confronted with the full force of its reality, their faith wavered. They continued to question who Jesus was. John Mark was writing during a time of growing persecution of the church. It may be that he was also thinking about the storms of controversy the church was encountering and the message of peace Jesus had for the church.

Jesus Demonstrated Authority over the Human Condition (Mark 5:1–8)

To the south and east of the Sea of Galilee is the region known as the Gerasenes. This is a less-populated area than to the west of the Sea. Gerasenes was also an area inhabited at the time by Gentiles rather than Jews.

Jesus and the disciples directed their boat to this region on the east side of the Sea (v. 1). Upon reaching the shoreline, and **when Jesus got out of the boat**, He was promptly met by **a man with an evil spirit** (v. 2). This man **came from the tombs**, where outcasts from society often lived. Many first-century tombs were large rooms carved in the stone, with separate areas in the back where bodies could be laid.

The evil spirit had endowed this man with extraordinary strength, to the extent that he could not be bound, **not even with a chain** (v. 3). **He had often been chained hand and foot, but he tore the chains apart and broke the irons on his feet.** His strength was such that **no one was strong enough to subdue him** (v. 4). Further, this man's habitual habit was to **cry out and cut himself with stones** (v. 5). He must have been a frightening and sad sight indeed.

While Jesus was still a distance from the man, the evil spirit recognized Him, and the man **ran and fell on his knees in front of him** (v. 6). This was not bowing in submission to Jesus, but rather cowering to His authority. The evil spirit, through the man, voiced loudly, **"What do you want with me, Jesus, Son of the Most High God?"** (v. 7). The evil spirit attributed Jesus with the highest name it could possibly give. It instantly knew who He was and the authority with which He came. It affirmed, as did the demon cast from the man at the synagogue (1:21–28) that Jesus was the Son of God.

Demonic possession afflicts people for evil purposes. Scripture records mental derangement (Matt. 8:28) and physical illness

(Mark 9:17–27) as two such purposes. But one cannot assume that all such illnesses are demon possession. Demon possession occurs only when willful consent on the part of the host has been given, when a deliberate choice has been made. Evil spirits are damaging to the one possessed by them, harmful to others around, and have ultimate possessive power of their host. But, as this Scripture and others clearly indicate, they are no match for the authority and power of God. Christ's authority over the power of evil is complete and offers whole restoration.

This Scripture passage further describes the horrible destruction that comes with demon possession, and by implication the destruction that comes from sin itself. Sin is insanity, which the man demonstrated in his deranged state of hideous, uncontrollable screams that resonated among the hills of the region. Sin is self-destructive, which we see as the man attempted time and again to cut himself with stones.

The demon knew he had met his match and begged Jesus not to **torture** him (5:7). Jesus addressed the demon, not the man, in His response with the command, **"Come out of this man"** (v. 8) and demanded that it identify itself. The demon responded that its name was "Legion . . . for we are many" (v. 9). Legion, which was a garrison of three thousand to six thousand Roman soldiers, may have been the actual number of demons torturing this man. Though the demons "begged Jesus again and again not to send them out of the area" (v. 10), they groveled only for mercy, continuing in their refusal to submit to Jesus' authority.

The Man and the Crowd Responded with Amazement (Mark 5:15–20)

After Jesus cast out Legion from the man from the tombs, the people in the town and countryside gathered to see what had happened. Just as on the west side of the Sea, word of Jesus' miracle spread and the crowd turned out for the show.

When the town saw Jesus, they also encountered **the man who had been possessed by the legion of demons, sitting there, dressed and in his right mind** (v. 15). Verses 15–20 should be carefully contrasted with verses 1–5. Notice the significant change that occurred in the man now free from demonic control. The man, created in the image of God, was restored by the Creator himself. Humanity is not intended to be wretched in the debauchery and control that Satan attempts to exert, but humanity is designed to live life reflective of the Creator's image. Salvation is all about restoring humanity to the fullness God intended: a whole humanity complete in relationship with the Creator, with other members of the human race, and with self. Too often Christians settle for partial and not whole salvation.

Upon seeing the man, **they were afraid** (v. 15). Their fear was probably the result of shocked surprise. They knew the man who had roamed the tombs, perhaps even meeting him from time to time as they journeyed outside the city. They knew his life of howling in the hills and self-destruction. Now he appeared fully clothed, and with his senses about him. Who would have the authority to bring about such change in the life of this man?

WORDS FROM WESLEY

Mark 5:15

And they were afraid—It is not improbable they might otherwise have offered some rudeness, if not violence. (ENNT)

Then they heard the story firsthand from the eyewitnesses, both of the man and the pigs (v. 16). Perhaps they could handle the story of the man, but the pigs were their livelihood. How could they possibly allow someone with this kind of authority to wreak further havoc in their town? Drowned pigs do not make good bacon! So they **began to plead with Jesus to leave their region** (v. 17). These Gentiles were not yet ready for Jesus' message and refused to welcome Him there.

Respecting their wishes, and not forcing himself upon them, Jesus got into the boat to leave. But the man whom Jesus had freed from the demons **begged to go with him** (v. 18). He was undeterred by the poor reception his town had given Jesus. He wanted to hear and experience more of this man from Galilee who had freed him from the Enemy.

But Jesus refused, and asked the man to complete another calling: **"Go home to your family and tell them how much the Lord has done for you, and how he has had mercy on you"** (v. 19). Go and spread the message of your divine healing to others. These people, the Gentiles of the Gerasenes, would not have been anticipating a messiah in the same way that the Jews of the Galilee synagogues should have been anticipating one. In fact, it would be entirely appropriate to say that this man was the first missionary to the Gentiles, twenty years before the apostle Paul received his Macedonian call (Acts 16).

WORDS FROM WESLEY

Mark 5:19

Tell them how great things the Lord hath done for thee—This was peculiarly needful there, where Christ did not go in person. (ENNT)

So the man followed Jesus' direction **and began to tell in the Decapolis how much Jesus had done for him** (Mark 5:20). The man must have been enthusiastic and effective in his telling, for **all the people were amazed** (v. 20). Later, in Mark 7:31, we see Jesus again venturing into the land of the Gerasenes, and then He is greeted much more warmly.

The **Decapolis** (5:20) refers to the ten cities and their surrounding area, nine of which lay to the east of the Jordan River and the Sea of Galilee. This was largely Gentile territory. Historically, these ten cities had become Greek because of the conquering of Alexander the Great, but later were captured by the Maccabees, and in 63 B.C. by Rome. They continued to be prominently Greek (Gentile) in culture, and because of their distance from Rome and unique culture, had banded together in a sort of consortium for mutual military and other interests.

DISCUSSION

Some people are fair-weather friends, but Jesus is a true friend, who walks alongside us in every stormy trial.

1. How do you explain the fact that Jesus was able to sleep during a ferocious storm?

2. What do you learn about Jesus from the way He handled the storm?

3. What storms in life do you think are most threatening to believers? To you?

4. What do you learn about the disciples from your study of Mark 4:38–41? Why do you agree or disagree that believers now, including yourself, are like the disciples?

5. Why do you agree or disagree that some forms of deviant behavior are influenced by demons?

6. What changes do you expect to see in the life of a person who experiences spiritual cleansing?

7. Is it easier to tell friends or family members about Jesus? Why?

PRAYER

Lord, keep us courageous when it comes to resisting the powers of darkness that are bent on our destruction. Keep us aware that You hold the leash on evil and that nothing can happen to us apart from Your permission and full awareness.

6

A BREAK WITH TRADITION

Mark 7:5–23

God requires a pure heart.

Thomas K. Beecher disdained all forms of deceit. After becoming exasperated with a clock in his church that was either too fast at times or too slow, he hung a sign on the wall above it. "Don't blame my hands," the sign announced, "the trouble lies deeper."

Human beings do wrong because the trouble lies deeper than what we see on the surface. The heart is at the core of every sin. This study reveals how Jesus exposed the hypocrisy of religious teachers and pointed to the heart as the source of all uncleanness.

COMMENTARY

The passage for this study comes near the middle of Mark's gospel. It has been preceded by sections dealing with Jesus' authority over the demonic, the diseased, and the dead. He calmed the storm, walked on water, and fed thousands, demonstrating His authority over nature. However, all was not well. John the Baptist had recently been beheaded, and Jesus had not been well received in His hometown. As chapter 7 opens, some Pharisees and teachers of the law had come north from Jerusalem to the western shores of the Sea of Galilee to observe what was happening. As they watched, they saw that some of Jesus' disciples were eating with unwashed hands, a no-no for strict Jews. Mark's explanatory parenthesis in 7:3–4 is not in the account of this same incident in Matthew 15; its presence here is for Mark's mostly Gentile audience. Matthew's Jewish audience needed no explanation because they knew of the Pharisees' rules about washings.

The Pharisees Questioned Jesus (Mark 7:5)

The Pharisees and teachers of the law asked Jesus, "Why don't your disciples live according to the tradition of the elders instead of eating their food with 'unclean' hands?" (v. 5). **The tradition of the elders** is a reference by the Pharisees to the Pentateuch in general, and in this case specifically to the various laws in Leviticus about clean and unclean. In addition to the Mosaic law, some scribes around the time of Ezra and beyond the end of the Old Testament began to apply and interpret the law for specific situations in ways that actually hid the great concepts of the Ten Commandments and their bedrock principles behind the fog of case-by-case application, as seen later in this passage. The two most well-known of these various traditions of interpretation were Hillel and Shammai, who often disagreed with one another.

The washing of hands and utensils eventually became not a matter of hygiene, as in Leviticus 11–15, but more of a ceremonial tradition that kept growing in complexity.

Jesus Responded from Their Scriptures (Mark 7:6–8)

Jesus said, **"Isaiah was right when he prophesied about you hypocrites. . . . 'These people honor me with their lips, but their hearts are far from me. They worship me in vain; their teachings are but rules taught by men'"** (vv. 6–7). This quotation from the great prophet points to the lip service religious people often use to hide their darkened hearts. The parable of the good Samaritan is one possible example of this preoccupation to avoid the unclean in order to maintain ritual purity rather than meeting a fellow human being's need.

WORDS FROM WESLEY

Mark 7:6

What multitudes to God draw near
In forms devoid of life or power,
Usurp the sacred character,
Themselves instead of Christ adore!
From self their whole religion flows,
Their worship is all false and vain,
Who dare on simple souls impose
The doctrines, rules, and laws of men.
Thee, Lord, that I may serve aright,
Still let my heart approach to Thee,
Find in Thy will its whole delight,
And pant for all Thy purity.
The honour which Thou dost require,
The worship which Thou wilt approve,
Is following with an heart entire
The God of holiness and love. (PW, vol. 11, 4)

Jesus then called their fastidiousness what it was: **the traditions of men** (v. 8).

What is the essence of genuine faith in God? Certainly another prophet of Isaiah's own time got it right when he said, "He has showed you, O man, what is good. And what does the LORD require of you? To act justly and to love mercy and to walk humbly with your God" (Mic. 6:8). These criteria of goodness have little to do with water but much to do with eternal truth and are prophetic expressions of what the law essentially means. Ritual purity, while not unimportant, cannot compare to the purity of heart and intention that God intended when He gave the Decalogue to Moses at Mount Sinai. The comparison is one of mountains like "Love the Lord your God with all your heart and your neighbor as yourself," and molehills like "Now, Moses, wash your hands." Humanity has a cardiac problem, not a skin blemish. It is in that inner being that the evils lie, as Paul noted in Romans

7:14–25. Jesus trumped their criticism by quoting their own recognized authority, Isaiah—the greatest of the prophets. In quoting Isaiah, He went back to an earlier interpreter of the law than the rabbinic interpretations of Hillel and Shammai.

Jesus Drove the Point Further (Mark 7:9–13)

Next Jesus spoke to the Pharisees and teachers of the law about the trivializing of the Ten Commandments that the "tradition of the elders" had led them to embrace. God said, "Honor your father and mother." This commandment is the first of the commandments in the second table of the law, the first one to deal with our human relationships. Honoring parents is fundamental to all the rest of the commandments. To fail to honor them is like putting the first button on your shirt in the wrong hole. If you miss the first right place, then you miss all the rest of the right places. Not killing, not committing adultery, not stealing, not lying about others, and not coveting what belongs to others begin with respect of our own parents.

However, according to a custom that had grown up in the "tradition of the elders," if someone dedicated something to God and said **Corban** (v. 11) over it, then whatever had been dedicated to God was not available for further use, and nothing could change that commitment. Jesus pointed out that this custom was even used to evade the fifth commandment about honoring parents and could stand in the way of their humane care.

Washing and taking self-interested oaths are not at the heart of biblical faith, but care for people is a better indication of one's right relationship with God. Jesus made this point in another incident in which the legalists criticized the disciples for gleaning on the Sabbath. The Sabbath was also Jesus' favorite day to heal those diseased in spirit and body. Certainly laws have their place but not at the expense of acts that arise from human compassion, acts that honor both God and people. Cutting off aid to one's parents, denying food to the hungry, and failing to allow healing on the Sabbath were in opposition to the God who gave the law. **Thus you nullify the word of God by your tradition that you have handed down. And you do many things like that** (v. 13).

What Is Real Defilement? (Mark 7:14–23)

Jesus then began to speak to the crowd rather than just the Pharisees and their friends from Jerusalem: **"Listen to me, everyone, and understand this. Nothing outside a man can make him 'unclean' by going into him. Rather, it is what comes out of a man that makes him 'unclean'"** (vv. 14–15). Was Jesus pointing at the people who had come up from Jerusalem, the Pharisees, and teachers of the law?

What were they to make then of the laws of uncleanness in Leviticus 11–15 and other places (see, for example, Num. 19)? What are we to make of all those Jewish people since that time who have died a martyr's death rather than violate the statutes of uncleanness? During the Maccabean struggle, Jewish heroes died rather that eat pork. Did they die in vain? Jesus did not seem to be criticizing people for having sincere convictions that they feel honor-bound to keep. However, He did say that it is not external things that contaminate the human soul, but it is the soul itself that issues the evidences of its own contamination. The laws of clean and unclean were for the protection of people living in the wilderness. Those commands were both to honor God's command and to prevent epidemic destructions of the people who had made a covenant to honor Him. The moral and spiritual laws purify the soul. The laws of diet and health protect the body. These two aspects of law meet in the free and chosen obedience of the soul because of love for God and neighbor.

WORDS FROM WESLEY

Mark 7:15

There is nothing entering into a man from without which can defile him. — Though it is very true, a man may bring guilt, which is moral defilement, upon himself, by eating what hurts his health, or by excess either in meat or drink; yet even here the pollution arises from the wickedness of the heart, and is just proportionable to it. And this is all that our Lord asserts. (ENNT)

After he had left the crowd and entered the house, his disciples asked him about this parable (Mark 8:17). At this point, Jesus told His disciples that the real problem is not food in the stomach but rather a spiritually diseased heart. What goes into the stomach is not a problem; it passes out of the body. But the fundamental issues of relationship with God have to do with the heart. (*Spirit* could be substituted for *heart* at this point.)

Notice again that Mark gave an explanatory comment for his Gentile readers in the latter part of verse 19: **In saying this, Jesus declared all foods "clean."** Paul made this same point in his epistle to the Romans (Rom. 14). He said that the issue was not days and foods but obedience in one's conscience toward God.

Jesus said, **"What comes out of a man is what makes him 'unclean.' For from within, out of men's hearts, come evil thoughts, sexual immorality, theft, murder, adultery, greed, malice, deceit, lewdness, envy, slander, arrogance and folly. All these evils come from inside and make a man 'unclean'"** (Mark 7:20–23). Thirteen evils, and many more, are the symptoms of the real heart disease that separates people from God and from other people as well. The Christian doctrine of original sin has this great insight: One does not commit adultery and become an adulterer, but one is an adulterer in the heart, and therefore commits the act of adultery. The same can be said for all of these heart issues. The heart or spirit is the country of origin for all sin.

WORDS FROM WESLEY

Mark 7:20–23

Our Lord here teaches, that all evil thoughts, words, and actions, of every kind, flow out of the heart, the soul of man, as being now averse to all good, and inclined to all evil." (WJW, vol. 9, 425)

Paul, in Philippians 4:7, encouraged us to let God's peace guard our hearts and minds in Christ Jesus. This same Jesus warned His disciples not to be so anxious about washing hands and watching diets as noticing what comes out of our hearts as the indicators of our spiritual condition.

WORDS FROM WESLEY

Mark 7:21

"Out of the heart of man" (if at all) "proceed evil thoughts" (Mark 7:21). If, therefore, his heart be no longer evil, then evil thoughts can no longer proceed out of it. If the tree were corrupt, so would be the fruit: But the tree is good; the fruit, therefore, is good also; (Matt. 12:33); our Lord himself bearing witness, "Every good tree bringeth forth good fruit. A good tree cannot bring forth evil fruit," as "a corrupt tree cannot bring forth good fruit" (Matt. 7:17–18). (WJW, vol. 6, 17)

DISCUSSION

Adhering to religious traditions and rituals can be more important to some people than trusting in Jesus. The Pharisees and teachers of the law valued external religion and refused to believe in Jesus.

1. How does Mark 7:6–8 describe the actions of hypocrites?

2. How do you distinguish genuine Christianity from hypocritical religion?

3. Read Micah 6:8. How would a person's life show that he or she acted justly? Loved mercy? Walked humbly with God?

4. How would you define *religious legalism*? What kinds of religious legalism have you observed?

5. What evidences of sinful human nature have you observed in our culture?

6. Why do you agree or disagree that a person is not a sinner because he or she commits sins, but commits sins because he or she is a sinner?

7. How would you respond to someone who claims education can produce a utopian society?

PRAYER

Lord, give us the courage to let go of those traditions that get in the way of genuine fellowship with others and unhindered worship. Let us see what You see when it comes to what's truly in our hearts, and pull out any roots of bitterness that may have taken hold.

POWER THAT PRODUCES WHOLENESS

Mark 7:31–37; 8:14–25

Jesus has power to overcome the limitations
and diseases we face.

Fanny Crosby (1820–1915) lost her sight when she was six weeks old, but her disability did not deter her from writing eight thousand hymns that expressed her love for the Lord and her trust in Him. One of her hymns, "All the Way My Savior Leads Me," includes this testimony: "Heav'nly peace, divinest comfort, Here by faith in Him to dwell! For I know whate'er befall me, Jesus doeth all things well."

This study portrays Jesus as the compassionate healer and provider. Not surprisingly, those who witnessed His healing of a deaf mute remarked, "He has done everything well" (Mark 7:37). We will find ourselves in full agreement with their observation as we progress through this study.

COMMENTARY

Jesus was entering His third year of ministry. In His first year, He launched His teaching and healing ministry and began to gather followers. In His second year, He called twelve disciples to follow Him as He expanded His ministry. Toward the end of this year, Jesus began to experience rejection not only from religious leaders, but even from His own family. During His third and final year of ministry, this rejection only increased.

In these verses in Mark, Jesus was moving beyond His current scope of ministry by embarking on a journey into Gentile territory, where He ministered in many of the same ways He did to Jewish people. Reading these passages in Mark reminds us of the prophecy of Isaiah 49:6, which declared that the Messiah would be a light to the Gentiles.

Jesus Healed the Deaf and Mute Man (Mark 7:31–37)

Leaving Gennesaret (6:53), Jesus traveled north to **Tyre** and then **through Sidon** (7:31). Tyre was located in Phoenicia (modern-day Lebanon) to the north of Jesus' native Galilee. It is interesting to note that we have nothing recorded about His ministry there. Jesus then went southward to Decapolis, which was a district of ten cities on the northeast side of the Sea of Galilee. It was also a district where many Jews and Gentiles lived. It was there that Jesus performed another miraculous sign by healing **a man who was deaf and could hardly talk** (v. 32).

This man's friends were deeply concerned for him; they brought the man to Jesus and **begged him** to heal **the man** (v. 32). The first thing Jesus did was to take the man **aside, away from the crowd** (v. 33). He wanted close and personal contact with him. This is one of the few instances where Jesus removed a person from his or her environment before ministering to him or her.

WORDS FROM WESLEY
Mark 7:33

He put his fingers into his ears—Perhaps intending to teach us, That we are not to prescribe to Him (as they who brought this man attempted to do) but to expect His blessing by whatsoever means He pleases: even though there should be no proportion or resemblance between the means used, and the benefit to be conveyed thereby. (ENNT)

Jesus didn't just speak a word and heal the man even though He could have. Nor did He simply touch the man and make him whole. Instead, **Jesus put his fingers into the man's ears. Then he spit and touched the man's tongue** (v. 33). Mark said that Jesus **looked up to heaven and with a deep sigh** spoke the word, **"Ephphatha!" (which means, "Be opened!")** (v. 34). By looking to heaven, Jesus showed those watching that He was not relying on His own power, but was praying to the Father to perform this healing. As He looked to heaven, He drew the man's attention away from himself and to the One who had the power to transform his life.

Why did Jesus use this method to heal this man? He had not healed this way before. He had only to speak and the man would have been healed. He had only to touch the man, and the miracle would have been complete. Perhaps since this man could neither hear nor speak, Jesus showed him rather than told him what He was going to do. He wanted the man to activate his faith and understand the miracle He was about to perform.

Because of this man's encounter with Jesus, his **ears were opened, his tongue was loosened and he began to speak plainly** (v. 35). This miracle was instantaneous and complete. Not only could the man hear, but he could also be clearly understood as he spoke. His speech needed no rehabilitation.

WORDS FROM WESLEY
Mark 7:34

Ephphatha—This was a word of Sovereign Authority, not an address to God for power to heal, such an address was needless; for Christ had a perpetual fund of power residing in himself, to work all miracles whenever He pleased, even to the raising the dead. (ENNT)

After performing this healing, **Jesus commanded** the people **not to tell anyone** (v. 36). Again, Jesus did not want attention to be brought to himself. He still had work to complete and wanted nothing to interfere with His mission. Yet **the more he did so, the more they kept talking about it** (v. 36). Their excitement about this miracle compelled them to talk about it. And the more they talked about it, the more they wanted to tell the story. The **people were overwhelmed with amazement** and said, **"He has done everything well"** (v. 37).

If only the church could become this excited about the good news of the gospel. If only we would be convinced that Christ does everything well. Instead of being instructed to keep silent, we are commanded to take the message not only to those in our spheres of influence, but to the entire world. Yet how often do we remain silent about the wonderful things God has done in our lives? In this respect, we are dumb (speechless). It is time that we believers stop fearing others and declare the mighty works of God in our generation. It is time we get excited about the Lord we serve!

The Disciples' Spiritual Deafness and Blindness (Mark 8:14–21)

Preceding this passage, we find that Jesus repeated His miraculous feeding of a crowd. This time the count was four thousand. And just like the miracle of the feeding of the five thousand, again He had the disciples participate (8:1–10).

In response to this miracle, the Pharisees came to Jesus, tested Him, and asked for a sign from heaven (8:11–13). Obviously, feeding a crowd of five thousand and then feeding another crowd of four thousand was not enough. The signs of healing Jesus performed were not enough. In other words, nothing Jesus could do would be enough of a sign for them to embrace His message or convince them He truly was the Messiah.

According to Mark 8:13, Jesus and His disciples got into the boat and crossed over to the other side of the Sea of Galilee. As they were going, they realized that they **had forgotten to bring bread, except for one loaf** (v. 14). Obviously, this one loaf was not enough to satisfy all twelve disciples and Jesus.

Jesus used this incident as another opportunity to teach a spiritual truth. He **warned them** to **watch out for the yeast of the Pharisees and that of Herod** (v. 15). In using the comparison of leaven, Jesus was making a statement. Only a small amount of yeast will leaven a whole loaf of bread. Yeast in Scripture generally refers to evil. Like yeast permeates bread dough, evil affects the heart. A little evil can ruin our hearts.

We can gain an understanding of the yeast of the Pharisees in Mark 8:12. The Pharisees were seeking a sign from heaven to prove Jesus was the Messiah. In Luke 23:8, we find that Herod also was looking for a miraculous sign to prove who Jesus was. This yeast, the evil in their hearts, was the desire to see the miraculous in order to believe. Instead of exercising their faith, they demanded proof.

The disciples being dull of spiritual insight decided that Jesus was talking about physical bread. Jesus, perceiving this, asked them, **"Why are you talking about having no bread? Do you still not see or understand?"** (Mark 8:17). He drew their memories back to when He fed both the five thousand and the four thousand. Each time they retrieved more leftovers than what they had at first. Jesus was trying to help them discover who He was without seeking a sign from heaven.

Each of us comes to Christ through faith. No matter how many miraculous signs we might see, we cannot see Christ for who He is without faith. Generally, people who witness the miraculous without faith simply explain it away or reject it totally. The same kind of doubt that was in the hearts of the Pharisees and Herod could have destroyed what God was doing in the lives of these disciples. Jesus wanted their attention to be on Him and not on the miraculous things He was doing. He asks us to do the same today. He is looking for those who will seek His heart and not just His hand.

Jesus Healed the Blind Man at Bethsaida (Mark 8:22–25)

Another healing of Christ's took place at Bethsaida, which means "house of fish." It is located on the eastern bank of the Jordan River where it flows into the Sea of Galilee.

News of Jesus must have filled that town. For we see that **some people brought a blind man and begged Jesus to touch him** (v. 22). Jesus didn't choose to perform the healing there. Instead, He **took the blind man by the hand and led him outside the village** (v. 23). Why He did this is uncertain. There are only three incidents where Jesus withdrew from the people in the book of Mark in order to minister to them. He withdrew when He healed the deaf and mute man in chapter 7. He also withdrew when He healed Jarius's daughter (5:35–43), and He withdrew here when He healed this blind man.

WORDS FROM WESLEY
Mark 8:23

He led him out of the town—It was in just displeasure against the inhabitants of Bethsaida for their obstinate infidelity, that our Lord would work no more miracles among them, nor even suffer the person He had cured, either to go into the town, or to tell it to any therein. (ENNT)

Again, Jesus did not just speak a word or simply touch the man. Instead, He **spit on the man's eyes and put his hands on him** (8:23). The result was that the man had only a partial healing. He said, **"I see people; they look like trees walking around"** (v. 24). From this we surmise that his vision was blurry and out of focus. Scripture tell us that Jesus simply **put his hands on the man's eyes. Then his eyes were opened, his sight was restored, and he saw everything clearly** (v. 25). With a second touch from Jesus, the healing was complete.

This story raises some questions. First, why did Jesus decide to spit on the man's eyes? Jewish rabbis considered saliva to be a valid treatment for blindness. What was Jesus doing? Perhaps Jesus wanted to increase the man's faith. By having Jesus' saliva on his eyes, the man knew what to expect—a healing of his sight. Or perhaps Jesus wanted the man to see that a natural cure was insufficient. The saliva alone did not give him complete healing.

Second, did Jesus really fail the first time? What was He trying to accomplish by allowing this healing to take place gradually? We must remember that Jesus is not bound by any one method. Just because He uses a certain method with us does not mean He will act the same in everyone's life. He treats us individually. We cannot put Him into a box and expect Him to always move in the same way. According to Scripture, He heals in a variety of ways. Many times He brings healing in our lives gradually.

The placement of this miracle in Scripture is not accidental. We know that the disciples needed more understanding. This miracle is a picture of how their spiritual insight would come—not all at once, but by allowing Jesus to reveal himself more and more as they were able to receive that revelation. He works in our lives the same way. He teaches us line upon line, precept upon precept, until we have a greater understanding of Christ and His ways. By healing this man in this manner, God may be dramatically showing us that spiritual insight comes gradually, not like turning on a light switch in the soul.

The healing of the deaf and mute man and the healing of this blind man also draws our attention to the fact that it was easier for Christ to heal physical ears, mouths, and eyes than to bring spiritual understanding to His disciples. And although these miraculous healings excite our hearts, the greatest miracle occurred when Christ opened the eyes, ears, and hearts of His disciples. How many in the church today are as the disciples—dull of understanding of

God and His ways? May we allow the Lord to touch us in His way and in His time to bring us spiritual insight.

DISCUSSION

Sometimes the only way to reach a person's soul is to minister first to his or her physical needs. That's what Jesus did.

1. Read Mark 7:33. What event(s) has the Lord used to take you aside, away from the crowd, to be alone with Him? How would you describe those times?

2. Why would you say amen to the comment in Mark 7:37 that Jesus has done everything well?

3. What might have been Jesus' reason for commanding people to keep quiet about the healing of the deaf mute?

4. What do you believe was the main purpose of the feeding of the four thousand?

5. What did the Pharisees reveal about themselves by asking Jesus for a sign?

6. Hypothetically, if you could choose between signs and Scripture as foundational to your faith, which would you choose? Why?

7. What actions did Jesus take when He healed the blind man at Bethsaida?

8. What actions did Jesus take on your behalf that led to the removal of your spiritual blindness?

PRAYER

Lord, help us to never lose our amazement over the work You are doing in our lives and in the lives of those close to us. Let us never forget the ways You've delivered us in the past, especially when we need courage to face similar, perhaps bigger, challenges in the future.

QUESTIONS ONLY YOU CAN ANSWER

Mark 8:27—9:1

Jesus calls us to a life of discipleship.

Big questions confront all of us at times: What college should I attend? What occupation should I pursue? Who should I vote for in the next presidential election? Should I marry or remain single? If I choose to marry, what kind of future spouse should I look for? These are surely big questions, but the biggest questions each of us must answer concern the person and work of Jesus. Who is He, and why did He come to earth?

This study raises those questions and offers the right answers. Our destiny in this life and the next depends on our getting the answers right.

COMMENTARY

Mark 8:31—9:1 is pivotal in the gospel of Mark. Mark 1:1–15 introduces the entire book by quickly mentioning John the Baptist and Jesus' baptism and temptation. Mark immediately sets out to identify Jesus as the true Messiah, the Christ (1:16—8:30). Then he reveals the nature of the Messiah's mission. Jesus came to be the Suffering Servant, which culminates in His passion and crucifixion (8:31—15:47). Chapter 16 details the events of resurrection Sunday morning.

In Mark 8:31—10:52, the focus is on Jesus teaching His followers about His mission as the Messiah and their mission as His disciples. Jesus predicted His own suffering and death three times (8:31–33; 9:30–32; 10:32–34). After each prediction, there is a section on what it means to be a disciple of the Christ. Jesus taught His followers that (contrary to existing Jewish expectations) the Messiah's true mission was to suffer and die for His people. Then He taught them that true discipleship means complete commitment to Him and selfless service for others.

This week's study text concludes a section (Mark 7:31—9:1) that relates how Jesus healed individuals with perception problems— both physical and spiritual. In the area of Decapolis, east of the Jordan River, Jesus healed a deaf mute (7:31–37). Jesus had compassion on a hungry crowd, while the disciples could only see an unsolvable problem. He fed four thousand people with the seven loaves of bread His disciples had on hand (8:1–10).

Jesus then crossed to the district of Dalmanutha, on the western shore of the Sea of Galilee. The Pharisees there demanded a miraculous sign, and Jesus refused because of their insincerity (8:11–13). They refused to believe the miracles they had already seen. As Jesus and the twelve disciples crossed the Sea of Galilee heading to the village of Bethsaida on the northeast shore, Jesus confronted their failure to perceive the error of the Pharisees. He asked them, "Why are you talking about having no bread? Do you still not see or understand? Are your hearts hardened? Do you have eyes but fail to see, and ears but fail to hear? Do you still not understand?" (8:14–21).

Finally, outside the village of Bethsaida, Jesus healed a blind man (8:22–26). In the following verses, Jesus intended to heal the disciples' spiritual perception problems. He took them for a walk in the countryside.

Jesus' Identity (Mark 8:27–30)

Jesus and his disciples went on from Bethsaida **to the villages around Caesarea Philippi** (v. 27). Caesarea Philippi was situated near the northern boundary of Israel, 150 miles north of Jerusalem and thirty miles east of Tyre and the Mediterranean Sea. It had an elevation of about 1,150 feet above sea level, near the foot of Mount Hermon. It was an isolated place, making it easier for Jesus to talk to His disciples without interruption as they traveled.

On the way (as they were walking) **he asked them, "Who do people say I am?"** (v. 27). This was Jesus' first question in this conversation. He planned for their answers to provide Him with an opportunity to heal their hard hearts, blind eyes, and deaf ears (8:17–18). His ultimate goal in this private time with the Twelve was to remove from their minds any false ideas about His identity and mission.

Their answers reflect the ideas of Herod and others reported in Mark 6. The disciples **replied, "Some say John the Baptist"** (8:28), who would have had to have been raised from the dead because Herod had already beheaded him (Mark 6:16–40). The disciples also noted that **others** said Jesus was **Elijah**. Perhaps they believed Jesus was the forerunner of the Messiah since John the Baptist had denied being Elijah (John 1:19–27). They went on to say that **still others** believed Jesus was **one of the prophets** come back to life (Mark 8:28). Clearly, the people of Jesus' day did not think of Him as just another rabbi or religious leader.

"But what about you?" he asked. "Who do you say I am?" (v. 29). This was the key issue and the ultimate reason for this conversation. It did not matter in the end what others thought about Jesus. The answer to this question determined the success of Jesus' ministry to the Twelve. Jesus needed to convince His closest friends that He was the Messiah or all would be lost.

"But what about you? . . .Who do you say I am?" This question is still vitally important for each of us. It does not matter what the church teaches or what our friends and family believe about Jesus. We each must determine who Jesus is for ourselves. Our individual answers will determine the success of His ministry in our lives.

As the representative for the Twelve, **Peter answered, "You are the Christ"** (v. 29), literally, the Messiah, the Anointed One of God, the Redeemer prophesied in the Old Testament. This is the first time in the gospel of Mark that the title **Christ** appears since Mark 1:1. Peter's confession and the transfiguration (9:2–13) form the peak in the disclosure of Jesus' identity and a turning point in His ministry.

After praising Peter for receiving God's revelation (Matt. 16:16–19), **Jesus warned them not to tell anyone about him** (Mark 8:30). This strange command is a theme that runs through Mark's gospel (see 1:34, 44; 3:11–12; 7:36; 9:9). This high point of revelation came with an order to keep it secret. However, the reason becomes clear in the following verses. Jesus did not want human ideas about the Messiah to compromise His true calling to be the Suffering Servant and Savior of all humanity.

WORDS FROM WESLEY

Mark 8:30

He enjoined them silence for the present, 1. That He might not encourage the people to set Him up for a temporal king; 2. That He might not provoke the scribes and Pharisees to destroy Him before the time; and, 3. That He might not forestall the bright evidence which was to be given of His divine character after His resurrection. (ENNT)

Jesus' Mission (Mark 8:31–33)

Imagine how the disciples must have felt. God had revealed to them Jesus' identity. Their good friend was the Messiah, the promised Savior of Israel. They must have been thrilled beyond words. Then they may have been confused when He told them to keep His identity a secret. Their confusion must have deepened to outright chaos because Jesus **then began to teach them that the Son** of Man must suffer many things and be rejected by the elders, chief priests and teachers of the law, and that he must be killed and after three days rise again** (v. 31). **Must** indicates a divine necessity established on God's plan for Jesus. He told them He had to **suffer many things**. The Old Testament prediction of the Suffering Servant is found primarily in Isaiah 52:13—53:12.

He spoke plainly about this (Mark 8:32). Jesus' public teaching was mainly in parables (4:10–12), but the Twelve received clear coaching privately. However, **Peter took Jesus aside and began to rebuke him** (8:32). Peter rebuked Him because he thought Jesus had an imperfect understanding of the Messiah's mission. Nevertheless, Peter was the one with a misunderstanding of the Messiah's true mission. Again, he spoke as the representative of the Twelve. Peter could not reconcile the idea of the suffering messiah with the contemporary Jewish concept. In the popular thought of that day, there was only room for a doctrine of a victorious messiah. The Christ was to conquer all of Israel's enemies and make Jerusalem the capital of a worldwide empire. To Peter, as to any other Jew, the words *suffer* and *messiah* had nothing in common. No wonder he declared, "Never, Lord! . . . This shall never happen to you!" (Matt. 16:22).

But when Jesus turned and looked at his disciples, he rebuked Peter (Mark 8:33). Apparently, Jesus' love for His disciples empowered Him to resist this temptation. In the wilderness, Satan had tempted Jesus to take three different shortcuts to gaining the whole world. When Jesus refused to yield to his enticements, Satan left Him and waited for a more opportune time (Luke 4:13). Here he came again attempting to sidetrack Jesus from God's plan through Jesus' good friend. Once again, Jesus overcame the temptation.

"Get behind me, Satan!" he said. "You do not have in mind the things of God, but the things of men" (Mark 8:33). Peter was so wrong that Jesus **rebuked** him just as He had rebuked the unclean spirits in Mark 1:25. The disciples were thinking like the average person, seeing only the **things of men**. They failed to perceive the **things of God** and did not see Jesus from the divine perspective (8:33).

Jesus' Call (Mark 8:34—9:1)

Since Jesus **called the crowd** (v. 34) to join Him and His disciples, we know this teaching was not limited to the Twelve. His call to follow Him in a life of suffering extends to everyone who wants to live for God.

WORDS FROM WESLEY
Mark 8:34

And when he called the people—To hear a truth of the last importance, and one that equally concerned them all. *Let him deny himself*—His own will, in all things small and great, however pleasing, and that continually: *And take up his cross*—Embrace the will of God, however painful, daily, hourly, continually. Thus only can he follow Me in holiness to glory. (ENNT)

Jesus **said: "If anyone would come after me, he must deny himself and take up his cross and follow me. For whoever wants to save his life will lose it, but whoever loses his life for me and for the gospel will save it"** (vv. 34–35).

This is one of Jesus' obvious paradoxes. It calls for the voluntary sacrifice of a person's life for Christ. This command does not demand martyrdom in order to obtain eternal life. It demonstrates that all who follow Jesus must give their lives to Him completely. This kind of "death" results in the kind of life God created humans to enjoy.

The call to deny self does not mean to go without something we want or that we should look down on ourselves. To deny self means to give full control of our lives to Jesus. The person who carried a cross was on the way to his or her execution. It was a one-way trip. This is a great word picture. It describes the individuals who exchanged their independence for dependence on Jesus. They are ready to join Jesus in praying, "Not my will but yours be done" (Luke 22:42).

WORDS FROM WESLEY

Denying Self

The two grand hinderances of prayer, and consequently of faith, are self-love and pride: therefore our Lord so strongly enjoins us self-denial and humility.

"If any man will come after me, let him deny himself, and take up his cross daily, and follow me." And, "How CAN ye believe who RECEIVE HONOUR one of another, and seek not the honour which cometh from God ONLY?" Here, you see, pride is an insurmountable obstacle to believing. Yet the desire of praise is inseparable from our fallen nature. All we can do, till faith comes, is not to seek it; not to indulge our own will; not to neglect the means of attaining faith and forgiveness, especially private prayer, and the Scripture. (JCW, vol. 2, 277).

Jesus expanded on this call to complete commitment by eliminating two competing options. First, He pointed out that possessions cannot take the place of our souls. **What good is it for a man to gain the whole world, yet forfeit his soul? Or what can a man give in exchange for his soul?** (Mark 8:36–37). The word translated here as **soul** is the same Greek word translated as *life* in verse 35. No financial or material possession equals the cost of the life only God can give through Jesus.

Second, Jesus pointed out that popular acceptance in this life can disconnect us from the life God intends for us to experience. **"If anyone is ashamed of me and my words in this adulterous and sinful generation, the Son of Man will be ashamed of him**

when he comes in his Father's glory with the holy angels"
(v. 38). Our response to Christ in this life determines our eternal
destiny.

Then Jesus **said to** the crowd and His disciples, **"I tell you
the truth, some who are standing here will not taste death
before they see the kingdom of God come with power"** (9:1).
Some commentators believe the event Jesus called **the kingdom
of God come with power** is a reference to His crucifixion,
resurrection, ascension, or return.

Jesus' return has not happened and His original audience is all
dead, so He must have meant something else. His crucifixion was
public, so all the people could have seen it. Perhaps Jesus was
referring to the transfiguration, which was a visible encounter
with **kingdom . . . power** (9:1), observed six days later by Peter,
James, and John (9:2–13). The transfiguration was a preview of
both Jesus' resurrection and return.

WORDS FROM WESLEY

Mark 9:1

Till they see the kingdom of God coming with power—So it
began to do, at the day of Pentecost, when three thousand were
converted to God at once. (ENNT)

DISCUSSION

Who was Jesus, and what was His mission? Answers to these questions are crucial. A person's eternal destiny hinges on the correct answers.

1. According to Mark 8:28, what mistaken identifications did people assign to Jesus?

2. What identifications do some people attach to Jesus today? What is your opinion of each of these identifications?

3. Why do you agree or disagree that confessing Jesus as the Son of God is foundational to genuine faith?

4. What reason do you think Jesus had for commanding His disciples not to tell anyone that He is the Son of God?

5. Based on Mark 8:31, how do you know the crucifixion did not take Jesus by surprise?

6. Why was it so wrong of Peter to rebuke Jesus?

7. Under what circumstances might a Christian disapprove of God's plan?

8. According to Mark 8:36, what value does Jesus attach to a person's soul? How does this evaluation make you feel?

PRAYER

Lord, thank You for making Your expectations of us crystal-clear. You never promised us carefree lives; in fact, You told us that things will get harder because we have decided to follow You. Help us through those difficult times, and constantly remind us that You are sovereign of all the details of our lives.

9

GLORY FOR THE DAILY GRIND

Mark 9:2–7, 14–24

God hears us even when our faith is weak.

Movies about superheroes net Hollywood filmmakers hundreds of millions of dollars. Crowds rush to theaters to watch the exploits of Superman, Spiderman, and Batman. Many fans dress to look like their favorite superhero. They buy posters and mementos in their honor, and they talk frequently about their favorite superhero. Does such loyalty put Christians to shame? After all, superheroes are make-believe, whereas Jesus is real, personal, glorious, and compassionate.

This study focuses on Jesus' transfiguration and subsequent identification with human need.

COMMENTARY

Mark 8 includes the pivotal point for the gospel of Mark. That is where Peter made his great confession that Jesus was the Christ, or Messiah. Following Peter's confession, Jesus began teaching His disciples that soon He would go to Jerusalem. There He would be killed and then rise from the dead after three days. Impulsive Peter "took [Jesus] aside and began to rebuke him" (8:32). According to Peter's understanding of the Messiah, Jesus was confused. Peter had confessed Jesus to be the Messiah who would establish a kingdom for the oppressed Jews, overthrowing the Romans. No doubt the other apostles understood the role of the Messiah just as Peter did, even though they let Peter do the talking.

Jesus then rebuked Peter severely. "Get behind me, Satan! . . . You do not have in mind the things of God, but the things of men" (8:33). And then Jesus explained to the whole crowd that His followers must be ready to die with Him, "But whoever loses his life for me and for the gospel will save it" (8:35). The way of Jesus is the way of the cross. The kingdom comes in glory for those who were not ashamed of Jesus and His teachings (8:36–38). However, Jesus went on to say that some standing there would "not taste death before they see the kingdom of God come with power" (9:1). With their understanding of the Messiah and the kingdom of God, it is little wonder that the twelve disciples did not understand what Jesus was teaching them until it was fulfilled. As a cautionary note for us today, perhaps the same is true for most prophecies—we may not fully understand them until after they are fulfilled.

Our study in Mark 9 seems to reveal a partial fulfillment of Jesus' words. Many commentators have suggested that the transfiguration was a fulfillment, as Peter, James, and John did "see the kingdom of God come with power" on the mountain. But it was not yet the earthly power they had expected. Years later Peter still remembered the event: "We did not follow cleverly invented stories when we told you about the power and coming of our Lord Jesus Christ, but we were eyewitnesses of his majesty. For he received honor and glory from God the Father when the voice came to him from the Majestic Glory, saying, 'This is my Son, whom I love; with him I am well pleased.' We ourselves heard this voice that came from heaven when we were with him on the sacred mountain" (2 Pet. 1:16–18).

Jesus' Glory Was Revealed in the Transfiguration (Mark 9:2–7)

What was the purpose of the transfiguration? We may not know the depth of God's purposes in this supernatural event, but several possibilities can be suggested. Two that seem obvious are that it occurred to encourage Jesus for the trying days that lay ahead and to confirm Jesus' identity and mission to the apostles. As stated in the introduction, it can also be understood to fulfill Jesus' promise in Mark 9:1 that some standing there would "see the kingdom of God come with power." Without a doubt, these three purposes were fulfilled on the mountain.

The location of the Mount of Transfiguration is unknown. However, tradition holds that it was Mount Tabor. The *NIV Study Bible* in its note on Luke 9:28 suggests Mount Hermon as a more likely location. Mount Tabor is southwest of the Sea of Galilee, some forty to forty-five miles from Caesarea Philippi where Peter made his great confession. Also, Mount Tabor is only eighteen hundred feet high. Mount Hermon is much closer to Caesarea Philippi, ten to twelve miles away, and nine thousand feet high. Thus, Mount Hermon seems to fit better the scriptural context and the description of the location. It was **a high mountain, where they were all alone** (Mark 9:2). Nevertheless, we cannot be certain of the location.

WORDS FROM WESLEY

Mark 9:2

By themselves—That is, separate from the multitude: *Apart*—From the other apostles: *And was transfigured*—The Greek word seems to refer to the form of God, and the form of a servant (mentioned by St. Paul, Phil. 2:6–7) and may intimate, that the divine rays, which the indwelling God let out on this occasion, made the glorious change from one of these forms into the other. (ENNT)

His clothes became dazzling white, whiter than anyone in the world could bleach them. And there appeared before them Elijah and Moses, who were talking with Jesus (vv. 3–4). What a glorious sight appeared before the three disciples! Matthew,

Mark, and Luke all record the event. Mark alone tells us that Jesus' clothes were **whiter than anyone in the world could bleach them** (v. 3). Both Matthew and Luke add that His facial appearance was changed. "His face shone like the sun, and his clothes became as white as the light" (Matt. 17:2). "As he was praying, the appearance of his face changed, and his clothes became as bright as a flash of lightning" (Luke 9:29). Luke adds some additional details. "Peter and his companions were very sleepy, but when they became fully awake, they saw his glory and the two men standing with him" (Luke 9:32). There is little doubt that Peter and his companions were startled awake by what they saw. Luke also says that Moses and Elijah "spoke about his departure, which he was about to bring to fulfillment at Jerusalem" (Luke 9:31). Mark may allude to this conversation later: "They kept the matter to themselves, discussing what 'rising from the dead' meant" (Mark 9:10).

WORDS FROM WESLEY

Transfigured, Mark 9:2

How glorious the body of Christ is, we may guess from His transfiguration. St. Peter, when he saw this, when our Lord's face shone as the sun, and His raiment became shining and white as snow, was so transported with joy and admiration, that he knew not what he said. When our Saviour discovered but a little of that glory which He now possesses, and which in due time He will impart to His followers, yet that little of it made the place seem a paradise; and the disciples thought that they could wish for nothing better than always to live in such pure light, and enjoy so beautiful a sight. "It is good for us to be here: Let us make three tabernacles;"— here let us fix our abode for ever. And if they thought it so happy only to be present with such heavenly bodies, and to behold them with their eyes, how much happier must it be to dwell in such glorious mansions, and to be themselves clothed with so much brightness! (WJW, vol. 7, 481)

How did they know who the men speaking with Jesus were? Perhaps Moses and Elijah appeared in a manner that fit with the popular conceptions of that time, conceptions known to the three apostles. Or perhaps names were spoken in the conversation between Moses, Elijah, and Jesus. Again, that is a detail we are not given.

Peter said to Jesus, "Rabbi, it is good for us to be here. Let us put up three shelters—one for you, one for Moses and one for Elijah" (v. 5). Peter was so frightened that he didn't know what to say, but he spoke anyway. It was a time to bow in awe and worship rather than to speak. However, Peter apparently suggested that they stay awhile, that they build temporary housing for Jesus, Moses, and Elijah right there on the mountain. Sometimes we may talk when we should be listening lest we miss God's words to us. Not this time! **Then a cloud appeared and enveloped them, and a voice came from the cloud: "This is my Son, whom I love. Listen to him!"** (v. 7). An awesome and frightening vision suddenly became even more frightening as a cloud enveloped them. God's voice from the cloud was unmistakable as He once again affirmed Jesus as His Son whom He loved. **Listen to him!** Peter did not know what to say, but Jesus did.

WORDS FROM WESLEY

Mark 9:7

There came a (bright, luminous) *cloud, overshadowing them—* This seems to have been such a cloud of glory, as accompanied Israel in the wilderness, which, as the Jewish writers observe, departed at the death of Moses. But it now appeared again, in honour of our Lord, as the great prophet of the church, who was prefigured by Moses. *Hear ye him—*Even preferably to Moses and Elijah. (ENNT)

A Boy with an Evil Spirit and the Disciples' Unbelief (Mark 9:14–24)

When they came to the other disciples, they saw a large crowd around them and the teachers of the law arguing with them (v. 14). Coming down the mountain, they soon encountered the world of people—people who were sometimes disagreeable. The remaining disciples were surrounded by a crowd and by teachers of the law. They were arguing with the teachers of the law, but the disciples seemed to be in a situation that was over their heads. When Jesus appeared, the people **were overwhelmed with wonder and ran to greet him** (v. 15). Why were they **overwhelmed with wonder** or "greatly amazed," as the RSV translates it? Maybe it was just because they were glad to finally see Jesus, whom they hoped would solve the immediate problem. Or possibly Jesus still had remnants of the transfiguration glory similar to Moses' experience after being with God on Mount Sinai (see Ex. 34:29–35).

"What are you arguing with them about?" (Mark 9:16). Jesus was concerned when He saw the scene around the disciples. He quickly learned what the problem was. A man cried out from the crowd saying that he had brought his son to be delivered from a **spirit that** had **robbed him of speech** (v. 17). The man described how his son behaved when under attack, and then continued: **"I asked your disciples to drive out the spirit, but they could not"** (v. 18). The ensuing argument was what confronted Jesus as He arrived. Likely, the teachers of the law had mocked the disciples for their inability to help the father and his afflicted son.

"O unbelieving generation," Jesus replied, "how long shall I stay with you?" (v. 19). Jesus chided the disciples for their unbelief. He knew He would soon be leaving them and their period of training would be over. His words sounded a bit exasperated. After all the miracles the disciples had seen and had even performed themselves (Mark 6:13), they still did not have enough faith to meet this need. The chiding may have been for others besides the disciples as well, for Jesus was concerned for anyone who did not believe. However, Jesus did have the solution to the problem: **"Bring the boy to me"** (9:19). Through faith, the disciples could have already brought the boy to Jesus before He ever arrived on the scene, but they had failed. How often do those words echo down through the years as we of little faith try to solve our problems on our own? "Bring them to me" is a message for us today just as it was for the disciples then.

So they brought him. When the spirit saw Jesus, it immediately threw the boy into a convulsion. He fell to the ground and rolled around, foaming at the mouth. Though they brought the boy to Jesus, the problem of unbelief had not yet been resolved. The spirit threw the boy into one of his seizures. The description sounds similar to epilepsy. Whatever the nature of the attack, **from childhood** (v. 21) it had been a problem for the boy. Any loving father would have been very distressed, just as this father was. But he had come to the right source for help.

Jesus asked about the history of the problem. The father answered that it was an affliction so severe that the boy's life was sometimes endangered: **"It has often thrown him into fire or water to kill him. "But if you can do anything, take pity on us and help us"** (v. 22). The father was desperate for help. The affliction his son experienced was out of control, and only a miracle could release him. The disciples had failed to exorcise the spirit. Jesus was his last hope. **"'If you can'?" said Jesus. "Everything is possible for him who believes"** (v. 23). Jesus did not turn him away. Very forcefully, Jesus asserted His power to do anything in response to faith.

After years of affliction and the failure of the disciples, the man was doubting but still had a little hope. He wanted to believe. **"I do believe; help me overcome my unbelief!"** (v. 24). From a plea like this, Jesus never turns away. He said, **"I command**

you, come out of him and never enter him again" (v. 25). And the spirit was gone. In spite of doubt, through Jesus, the boy was delivered.

WORDS FROM WESLEY

Mark 9:23–24

23. *If thou canst believe*—As if He had said, The thing does not turn on my power, but on thy faith. *I* can do all things: canst *thou* believe?

24. *Help thou mine unbelief*—Although my faith be so small, that it might rather be termed unbelief, yet help me. (ENNT)

What should we do when we doubt? We can turn to Jesus with as much faith as we can muster and ask Him to help us. An answer will come. The answer may come in a way that is different from what we expect, but it will come. Jesus does not always heal illness in the present, but he will always bring spiritual healing in response to faith, and ultimately He will bring healing to the body even if it is through death and resurrection. We can be thankful for a God who hears a prayer like this father's: **I do believe; help me overcome my unbelief!** (v. 24). What wonderful assurance that God hears us even when our faith is weak!

DISCUSSION

Occasionally, the people of Israel saw God's glory in the tabernacle. When Jesus tabernacled on earth, He revealed His glory to three of His disciples on a mountaintop.

1. What purpose do you think the transfiguration served? Defend your answer.

2. Why do you think Jesus showed His glory to Peter, James, and John instead of to all His disciples?

3. Why do you agree or disagree that Jesus' glory came from within and not from an external source?

4. Why is it significant that Moses and Elijah talked with Jesus about His imminent death?

5. The three disciples recognized Moses and Elijah. Why do you agree or disagree that believers will recognize one another in heaven?

6. Do you think there is hero worship among Christians? Explain. How does Mark 9:7 address this issue?

7. Jesus and the disciples left the mountain and found an urgent need below. Do you think a Christian might be so heavenly minded that he or she is no earthly good? Why or why not?

PRAYER

Lord, sometimes we can be impulsive like Peter, saying things we shouldn't because we don't know what to say. Help us keep guard over our tongues. And Lord, if we are struggling with any doubts, lead us to mature believers to help us resolve them, so that our faith might grow even stronger.

THE IMPACT OF PERSONAL CHOICES

Mark 9:42—10:12

Personal choices make a public impact.

Susanna Wesley, the mother of John and Charles Wesley, gave birth to nineteen children. Nine of her children died in infancy, but Susanna Wesley never abandoned her faith in the Lord. She devoted herself to the Lord and gave each of her children love and encouragement. Every day, after holding personal devotions, she prayed with her children and led them in singing the psalms. Obviously, she viewed the home as the training ground from which her children would emerge as servants of the Lord.

This study gives us an opportunity to take a serious look at our home lives. It gives us God's perspective on children and marriage.

COMMENTARY

We often become very legalistic when it comes to certain issues, issues like the topic of our study today: divorce. Regarding divorce, attention to the letter of the law is certainly appropriate, but Jesus was always concerned about broader issues than just rules by themselves. The Pharisees, on the other hand, seemed to focus on the laws themselves—do what the law says whatever the consequences. Clearly, Jesus included consequences as well as rules when He said the greatest commandment was to love God and neighbors (Mark 12:28–31).

In this study, the primary focus is related to divorce and remarriage (Mark 10:1–12). Jesus' statements about the topic have often been taken as simple rules that are black and white.

In the context immediately preceding these statements, however, Jesus made it clear that there are broader implications related to marriage and divorce (Mark 9:42–50). Modern sociological studies make some of those broader implications clear as well. Often "little ones" are damaged the most by marital conflict and divorce. Some children are scarred for life because of parental choices. For the thoughtful Christian, divorce and remarriage are not simply legal choices. There are issues far more important than the question of whether it is allowed to divorce and remarry. There are souls at stake—not just the souls of the spouses involved, but those of children and other family members as well.

However, the gospel message is not a message of judgment and condemnation but of hope. Through Christ, forgiveness and healing can be found. Nevertheless, the other side of the gospel message is a warning to those who ignore the God's law and the gospel call. Our choices and actions do have both temporal and eternal consequences.

Then there is the question of how the church should deal with these issues. Certainly the church should strive to have a positive impact on the morality of society and more particularly on the morality of its members. A certain amount of church law seems to be needed, but the church's primary goal should always be redemptive rather than judgmental. Can we maintain that tension in a world of no-fault divorce? At a minimum, it seems we should work to change laws that almost seem to welcome divorce on a whim. Within our churches, we can also plan and implement better support for marriages through education and discipleship. May God help us understand His message for us today as we live in a world where the traditional family is under intense pressure.

If Anyone Causes One of These Little Ones Who Believe in Me to Sin (Mark 9:42)

Jesus had just said that "anyone who gives you a cup of water" in His name would be rewarded (9:41). Now He turned to the negative side. Causing **little ones who believe in** Jesus **to sin** is a grave offense. He said it would be better to die an awful death than to cause a little one to sin. Who are the little ones? Certainly children may be classified thus. And who has more influence over children than their parents? The warning may be for others as well, but surely it is a message for parents. Do we cause our children to sin? What kind of example do we set before them? Most parents try hard to set good examples for their kids! Still, most would welcome do-overs if given the opportunity. Thank God that perfection in living is not what is required. Rather, consistent effort to follow God's way is what is expected. Most of all, thank God for grace.

Both Matthew and Luke add words of Jesus to indicate that things that cause people to sin must come, but woe to the person through whom they come (Matt. 18:7; Luke 17:1). The world is marred by sin, but as believers our duty is to avoid the practice of sin. We must so strive. Through God's grace we are enabled to set good examples for children, not just our own, to follow.

Better for You to Enter the Kingdom of God Marred (Mark 9:43–49)

In the next several verses, Jesus gave additional exhortation that we take sin very seriously. Some have taken Jesus' words literally and actually mutilated themselves. The fact is that one's hand, foot, or eye does not cause a person to sin. Rather the problem lies in the heart, where sin is born. Jesus was using hyperbole here, and the extreme comparison suggests that we must take sin seriously, indeed. Sin has terrible consequences.

WORDS FROM WESLEY

Mark 9:43

And if a person *cause thee to offend*—(The discourse passes from the case of offending, to that of being offended) if one who is as useful or dear to thee as an hand or eye, hinder or slacken thee in the ways of God, renounce all intercourse with him. This primarily relates to persons, secondarily to things. (ENNT)

Does the passage actually mean that we will take our handicaps with us into the next life? Will the blind still be blind? Will the lame still be lame? Obviously, it could mean exactly that, but Jesus is likely still speaking in metaphors rather than stating facts about our bodies in the next life. It seems clear from this passage that hell (*gehenna*) will be awful, and in hell, dying will be without end. The destructive worm lives on; the fire burns on. Adam Clarke suggested that **salted with fire** (v. 49) may indicate that the person being punished will be preserved and not destroyed by the fire.

WORDS FROM WESLEY

Mark 9:44

Where their worm—That gnaweth the soul, (pride, self-will, desire, malice, envy, shame, sorrow, despair) *dieth not*—No more than the soul itself: *And the fire* (either material, or infinitely worse!) that tormenteth the body, *is not quenched* for ever. (ENNT)

Though many questions may remain about this passage, it is clear that we should avoid sin and most certainly avoid causing little ones to sin. Any hardship on earth is better than the punishment ahead for the sinner. God forbid that we should set an example of carelessness toward sin. Others will be affected by our example.

Have Salt in Yourselves (Mark 9:50)

Jesus also said His followers are the salt of the earth (Matt. 5:13). By implication in Mark 9 and Matthew 5, we can lose that saltiness. Believers must maintain their relationship with Jesus by following His ways and being **at peace with each other** (Mark 9:50). Certainly this exhortation applies in the family setting.

WORDS FROM WESLEY

Mark 9:50

More largely this obscure text might be paraphrased thus:

As every burnt offering was salted with salt, in order to its being cast into the fire of the altar, so every one who will not part with his hand or eye, shall fall a sacrifice to divine justice, and be cast into hellfire, which will not consume, but preserve him from a cessation of being. And on the other hand, every one, who, denying himself and taking up his cross, offers up himself as a living sacrifice to God, shall be seasoned with grace, which like salt will make him savoury, and preserve him from destruction for ever.

As *salt is good* for preserving meats, and making them savoury, so it is good that ye be seasoned with grace, for the purifying your hearts and lives, and for spreading the savour of my knowledge, both in your own souls, and wherever ye go. But as salt if it loses its saltness is fit for nothing, so ye, if ye lose your faith and love, are fit for nothing but to be utterly destroyed. See therefore that grace abide in you, and that ye no more contend, *Who shall be greatest.* (ENNT)

Question of Divorce (Mark 10:1–2)

Once again the Pharisees asked a question trying to trap Jesus through His words. The question they asked was controversial in their day and remains so in ours: **Is it lawful for a man to divorce his wife?** (v. 2). Divorce was legal in Jesus' day as it is today. So legally, the answer to their question was yes. The deeper issue, however, was whether divorce is right, moral, and approved by God.

Jesus' Question and Pharisees' Response (Mark 10:3–4)

As with any moral dilemma, the first thing needed is a clear statement of the facts. So Jesus asked the Pharisees what Moses had commanded. The Pharisees replied, citing part of Moses' statement from Deuteronomy 24:1–4: "If a man marries a woman who becomes displeasing to him because he finds something indecent about her, and he writes her a certificate of divorce, gives it to her and sends her from his house, and if after she leaves his house she becomes the wife of another man . . . then her first husband, who divorced her, is not allowed to marry her again after she has been defiled." Divorce was permitted by Moses, but hardly commanded. Pharisaic legalism had gone on to interpret "something indecent." The school of Hillel said it could be almost anything that displeased the husband. The school of Shammai said it meant adultery (*Interpreter's Bible Dictionary*, vol. 1, p. 859). The question was designed to entangle Jesus in the controversy, but He sidestepped the issue.

Hard Hearts (Mark 10:5)

Jesus said the passage in Deuteronomy was not a command Moses gave, but a concession to the people because their **hearts were hard** (v. 5). As many others have done, the Pharisees seem to have taken a reluctant exception as full authorization for divorce. Precedent can be a dangerous thing!

What God Has Joined Together (Mark 10:6–9)

Jesus quoted the fundamental principle for marriage that was first given in Genesis 1:27. The allowance of divorce by Moses was a concession to human failure. The ideal was stated at the beginning: **the two will become one flesh** (Mark 10:8). This being the case, Jesus said, the spouses are one flesh and should not be separated by anyone. Every divorce is a violation of the original ideal. Human sin is always involved in divorce. Certainly there may be occasions when divorce seems the lesser of the evils involved in complex human relations, but that does not negate the ideal of one flesh.

WORDS FROM WESLEY
Mark 10:6

From the beginning of the creation—Therefore Moses in the first of Genesis gives us an account of things from *the beginning of the creation*—Does it not clearly follow, that there was no creation previous to that which Moses describes? *God made them male and female*—Therefore Adam did not at first contain both sexes in himself: but God made Adam, when first created, male only; and Eve female only. And this man and woman He joined together, in a state of innocence, as husband and wife. (ENNT)

What God has joined together, let man not separate (v. 9). What constitutes the union described here? Some understand it to apply only to marriages performed within the church between believers. However, the statement in Genesis 1:27 seems more foundational that that. It seems to be a creation principle. Does sexual union constitute marriage and "one flesh"? Interpretation must be applied here, and there is room for more than one position. Paul indicated that even the sexual union with a prostitute is a "one flesh" union (1 Cor. 6:16–17). Whatever our interpretation of this question, it seems that there is little basis to treat non-Christian spouses as somehow different, as if they are not regulated by the Genesis statement and the words of Jesus. Sinful behavior is the cause of divorce, whoever is involved.

Having said that, does Jesus say that divorce is the unforgivable sin? Not at all! But to gloss over it as acceptable is certainly not in line with His words. In light of Mark 9:42–50, it is clear that Christians (and everyone else) should take seriously any actions that damage families, and particularly actions that damage children. There is no question that divorce is harmful. But are there exceptions? Of course. When there is violence, there may be justified reasons. In Matthew 19:9, Jesus made an exception for adultery. Sin may make a marriage intolerable, but that never makes divorce good. For the sake of families, reconciliation, even after adultery, is a worthwhile goal. Cases of persistent unfaithfulness or other habitual sin must be considered on an individual basis. Jesus was stating the ideal in answer to a specific question. It is not clear that He was laying down unalterable laws to be followed legalistically. It is clear that divorce on a whim or for romantic reasons is sinful. Marriage takes hard work and can be maintained in most, if not all, situations if there are two willing spouses.

WORDS FROM WESLEY
Mark 10:7

The sabbath and marriage were two ordinances instituted in innocency, the former for the preservation of the church, the latter for the preservation of mankind. It appears by *Matt.* 19:4, 5 that it was God himself who said here, a man must leave all his relations to cleave to his wife; but whether He spake it by *Moses* or by *Adam* who spake, ver. 23 is uncertain: It should seem they are the words of *Adam* in God's name, laying down this law to all his posterity. The virtue of a divine ordinance, and the bonds of it, are stronger even than those of nature. (ENOT, on Gen. 2:24)

Committing Adultery (Mark 10:10–12)

Jesus will not let anyone off the hook. Divorce is caused by sin, and remarriage is adultery against the former spouse. Can these principles be applied legalistically? Yes, and some do. Individuals and the church must prayerfully seek guidance related to these issues for individual cases. The gospel is clear that there is forgiveness for sin to the repentant. However, willful sinning

(unjustified divorce) with the plan to repent later is presumptu-
ous and dangerous. Such sins should always be condemned by
the church, but ultimately such sins are in God's hands.

How can the church manage this tension? We must condemn
the sin but be open to the sinner. At the same time, we must never
encourage the sin. For new believers, the gospel message seems
clear: Repent and be forgiven! For believers who rationalize
sinful behavior, the case is more complex. The church is always
a hospital for the sin-sick. Surely, though, we must take our stand
clearly in support of the principles Jesus stated regarding marriage and divorce. We must pray for the guidance of the Holy
Spirit even as we attempt to apply biblical principles to individual
cases.

DISCUSSION

Marriage and divorce are significant topics that involve highly personal choices, but the church, too, must choose to address these topics scripturally and lovingly.

1. Children of divorcing parents often suffer greater emotional pain than the parents. Based on Mark 9:42, how concerned is God when a child suffers?

2. How might a local church better prepare engaged couples for marriage? How can a local church do a better job of strengthening marriages? Why do you approve or disapprove of church-sponsored divorce recovery classes?

3. Why do you agree or disagree that the injunctions of Mark 9:43–48 should be taken literally?

4. How might "well-salted" believers flavor their family life? Their church life?

5. Do you think couples who rush into marriage are likely to rush into divorce? Defend your answer.

6. Do you agree that the Bible allows for divorce but does not condone it? Explain your answer.

7. If a church permits a divorced person to remarry, how can it also send an appropriate message about marriage to its young people?

PRAYER

Lord, help us to be creative in the ways we can be salt and light to the world that so desperately needs to be reconciled with You. Help us respond to hostility with grace and be patient with those who may mock us. May Your kindness, expressed through us, lead them to repentance.

THE ONLY WAY UP IS DOWN

Mark 10:32–45

We follow a leader who serves.

In his boxing career, Muhammad Ali often boasted, "I am the greatest." Perhaps he was—in boxing. The boast, however, is ingrained in the attitude of numerous athletes, politicians, and military men and women. Is it any wonder? Children are taught from preschool that they are special and can accomplish anything they desire. Athletes are advised to showcase their skills. Job applicants are told they must "sell" themselves.

But the "I am the greatest" attitude contradicts the attitude Jesus said His followers should have. This study shows that the only way up is down. God honors humility.

COMMENTARY

Jesus was headed toward Jerusalem, although He knew what it would cost. He repeatedly warned the disciples about the cross, but they failed to grasp His meaning. Their goals and ambitions clashed with His, so Jesus turned their misunderstanding into a key lesson about the values of the kingdom of God. Jesus did not condemn the disciples' ambition. Rather, He tried to reorient it into something of value to the kingdom.

The Way to the Cross (Mark 10:32–34)

Jesus was **leading the way ... to Jerusalem** (vv. 32–33). He did not show any sign of reluctance, although the cross was at the end of the journey. The **disciples were astonished, while** others **were afraid** (v. 32). The word *astonished*, or some form of it, occurs nine times, and the word *amazed*, seven times in the book of Mark. Jesus was always doing the unexpected, busily challenging the assumptions of His onlookers.

WORDS FROM WESLEY

Mark 10:32

They were on the way to Jerusalem, and Jesus went before them: and they were amazed—At His courage and intrepidity, considering the treatment which He had himself told them He should meet with there: *and as they followed, they were afraid*—Both for Him and themselves: nevertheless He judged it best to prepare them, by telling them more particularly what was to ensue. (ENNT)

They **were astonished** (v. 32) as they watched Jesus walk ahead of them. We can visualize Jesus in front of them at a certain distance. It was as if to show that the disciples were not just physically separated, but also mentally and emotionally separated from the heart of Jesus. Perhaps His followers already detected that something difficult and disastrous was about to occur.

These two reactions, astonishment and fear, often describe what we sense when we walk with Jesus. We are either astonished (and excited) at what He is doing in our lives, or lack trust in Him and fear where He might be leading us. In another situation, in Mark 4, Jesus asked the disciples point blank, "Why are you so afraid? Do you still have no faith?" He said that fear and faith cannot coexist. When we walk with Jesus, we need to look to Him in faith. We will indeed be continually amazed and astonished at Him, or else we will be walking in fear. Jesus' presence cannot leave us indifferent.

Jesus drew His followers together (and maybe the rest as well) to speak to them on the road to Jerusalem. Jesus was always in tune with His disciples. He could sense their emotions. We know from other accounts that there were more than the Twelve here. For example, Matthew states that Salome, the mother of James and John, was there. Also, as Passover was approaching, many travelers were probably on this well-used road. Considering how dangerous the road was, with bandits hiding behind sharp bends and on steep cliffs, it was safer to travel in numbers.

Going up to Jerusalem (Mark 10:33) refers to the geographical location of Jerusalem. It was located in the hill country of Judah. From the direction they were taking, from the Jordan valley, they would be going up. The road from Jericho to Jerusalem would take them from eight hundred feet below sea level to twenty-five hundred feet above sea level. As Jesus walked up the arduous inclines, there was much weighing on His heart. It was difficult both physically and emotionally.

In this aside conversation, Jesus referred to himself as the **Son of Man** (v. 33). Jesus used this title fifteen times in the book of Mark; all except one of the uses of this title were made after He declared that He would suffer and die on the cross.

Jesus detailed what would happen to Him with chilling clarity. His predictions made no sense to the disciples, and we can see this in how James and John tried to steer the subject to more personal matters. James and John took advantage of Jesus' speech to make a pressing request they hoped would further their interest in sharing His glory.

The Way to Glory (Mark 10:35–40)

From where we sit, our mouths may drop open at the apparent audacity of the two Sons of Thunder, James and John, as they tried to bait Jesus into making them some promises. They wanted Jesus to grant them **whatever** (v. 35) they asked for. But we need to pause for a moment and ask ourselves if their request is really so out of order. If it is bold, then our own hearts must come under the same scrutiny as well. Many of our own prayer lists and attitudes can resemble this same mentality. We pray as if Jesus should do exactly as we ask. Do we ever have that right?

It is intriguing that Jesus did not even get annoyed at their boldness. He heard them out. When they asked for prime seating at the soon-to-be-realized kingdom, He did not even chastise them. Did He see something in their hearts that we don't see? Once they made their request, Jesus did challenge them, though. They couldn't possibly understand what was to come, as we can see in their ready and eager response, **"We can"** (v. 39). **Cup** (v. 39), according to Wesley, relates to inward suffering, whereas **baptism** carries a sense of outward suffering (*John Wesley's NT Notes*, Albany: AGES Software, 1996, 150). Would they have been so enthusiastic if they had known what was ahead for each of them? Most certainly not, at this point; but something amazing happened to these Sons of Thunder after Pentecost. And the brothers did remain true to Jesus. Acts 12:2 reveals the death of James, the first of the disciples to face martyrdom. Many years later, John was exiled on the Island of Patmos. Tradition says that he had already suffered by being boiled in oil before his exile.

WORDS FROM WESLEY

Mark 10:38

Ye know not what ye ask—Ye know not that ye ask for sufferings, which must needs pave the way to glory. *The cup*—Of inward; *the baptism*—Of outward sufferings. Our Lord was *filled* with sufferings within, and *covered* with them without. (ENNT)

Jesus did not promise them these positions of honor. It is His Father who makes such decisions. It is always these "little" phrases of Jesus that catch us off guard. We see Jesus in complete submission to the authority of the Father. His obedience in all matters was always complete.

WORDS FROM WESLEY
Mark 10:40

Save to them for whom it is prepared—Them *who by patient continuance in well-doing, seek for glory, and honour, and immortality.* For these only eternal life *is prepared.* To these only He will *give it* in that day; and to every man his own reward, according to his own labour. (ENNT)

The Way to Lead (Mark 10:41–45)

In this passage, we see the other disciples' strong reaction to the requests of James and John. Now we know that Mark was writing this from Peter's memories. Peter was revealing his own emotion to be sure. He was one of the three in the inner circle, and it looked as if the other two were trying to push on ahead of him. But we also know that he was not alone. The ten heard and were indignant. But were they indignant about the same thing?

One idea is that they felt James and John were simply out of line. Just the fact that James and John approached Jesus with such a self-focused request was enough for indignation. "Didn't these years walking with Jesus teach them anything?" the ten may have wondered. Jesus never paraded in style, never owned a house, a mule, or any property. Some of the ten may have been just plain displeased that James and John were so completely self-seeking, much as we are when we read these words.

Another reason for their wrath may have been that some felt James and John got their request in before anyone else could. James and John were taking the places they themselves coveted; after all, there are only two places on either side of a throne. Jesus had virtually promised wealth in the previous section of Scripture, hadn't He? In Mark 10:29, Jesus said that no one who leaves everything for Him and the gospel will fail to receive a hundred times as much as what they left. In Matthew 19:28, Jesus even said the disciples would sit on twelve thrones. What did this idea of thrones mean to them? It could be tempting to embrace a gospel that promises power and authority and forget the lesson that came after: "But many who are first will be last, and many who are last will be first" (Matt. 19:30). Do we serve Jesus with hidden motives? Are we hoping to come out on top? Are we happy just as long as we are not last?

Whatever the source of their indignation, the disciples were filled with animosity toward the two brothers. Rather than allow this kind of destructive ill will to continue, Jesus called them all together once more. He needed to set the record straight. He was not recommending spiritual lordship over others. His kingdom is not about that. It is in fact directly opposed to anything of the kind. All Jesus had to do was to bring to mind the **Gentile** rulers (Mark 10:42). The disciples knew all about those men! The Jews had suffered oppression from foreign governments for centuries. There had been a long succession of Babylonian, Assyrian, Persian, Greek, and Roman oppressors. Maybe the pulses of some of the disciples quickened as they thought that Jesus would finally spread out His messianic plan against such. But all that came to a crashing halt with His words: **Not so with you** (v. 43). Like so many times in this gospel, Jesus hit them broadside with a radical kingdom principle that left them gasping for air. And we too are left to sheepishly examine our own ambitions. **"Whoever wants to become great among you must be your servant"** (v. 43). *Diakonos*, or **servant**, is the source of the English word *deacon*. It very clearly means to carry out the wishes of others. There can be no mistaking the idea of bending one's will to the desire of another. Surely, the disciples must have thought, "He did not mean to say *diakonos*; He meant to say something like *diktatwp* [dictator], right?" But Jesus did not leave any doubt as to what He meant. Jesus nailed it down so skillfully that they could not miss the implications.

Jesus didn't leave it there, though. For the stunning climax of this section of Scripture, Jesus showed them that He had served them and executed the orders of someone else. All these past years He had provided for them, ate what they ate, slept where they slept—and they lacked nothing. And now the greatest example of servanthood was what He was doing before their very eyes: heading to the cross. From the outset of this passage, Jesus was showing them true greatness in contrast to their own self-centeredness. From the start of His earthly ministry, He had done nothing but serve them and His Father. The ultimate test of this was still to come, as He would give up His life as a ransom for many, and more precisely, a ransom for them. Here is the key to the ambition question: There can be no desiring to serve or to be a slave for others without Jesus' ransoming our hearts back from the Evil One, who happens to be the great self-seeking one.

WORDS FROM WESLEY
Mark 10:45

The Son of man, the Man of woe,
Why did He leave the sky?
'T was all His business here below,
To serve us, and to die! (PW, vol. 11, 37)

The challenge for all of us is to allow Jesus to do just that, to ransom our hearts back from the Evil One. And then we must allow Him to transform our hearts, desires, and very ambitions to embrace the kingdom of God, replacing the earthly kingdom and its principles that we know so well. Will you?

DISCUSSION

Humble service on behalf of others may not rank high in the world's estimation, but Jesus gave it His highest commendation.

1. Knowing that Jesus was going to Jerusalem to die for our sins, what significance do you attach to the statement in Mark 10:32 that He was leading the way?

2. Why are fear and faith mutually exclusive? When did you experience fear but then replaced it with faith? What helped you make that transition?

3. What personal comfort and/or encouragement does Jesus' title "Son of Man" give you? Why?

4. Why do you agree or disagree that selfish ambition is diametrically opposed to God's will for His people? Is ambition itself wrong? Why or why not?

5. Why do you agree or disagree that the best model of leadership is servant leadership?

6. How do you account for the fact that so many churches lack an adequate number of volunteers?

7. What disasters have you seen that resulted from the misuse of authority? What blessings have you seen that resulted from servant leadership?

PRAYER

Lord, lead us to places where we can be free of all distractions and focus entirely on You. As we imitate Jesus in this way, whisper to our souls in the quiet moments of our lives.

THE BEGINNING OF THE END

Mark 13:1–13, 31–37

God is in control.

Four pastors were having a spirited discussion about future events. "I'm premillennial," the first declared. "I believe Jesus will return someday and establish His kingdom on earth."

"I'm postmillennial," the second pastor counseled. "I believe conditions on earth will improve until peace covers the planet, and then Jesus will return."

"Well," ventured the third pastor, "I'm amillennial. I believe the only kingdom that exists is present now where Jesus reigns in the hearts of His followers."

The fourth pastor spoke up. "I'm panmillennial. I believe everything will pan out just the way God plans."

Regardless of one's position about future events, it is good to know who holds the future. This study strengthens our confidence in the Lord as we examine His prophetic words.

COMMENTARY

Mark 13 is the longest sermon attributed to Jesus in Mark's gospel. It is commonly called the Olivet Discourse. This passage provides the transition in Mark's gospel from Jesus' earthly ministry to His passion narrative, which begins with the story of His anointing in 14:1–11, followed by the Last Supper in 14:12–26 and so on through the trial, crucifixion, and resurrection. The indication is that this was a private encounter, as in John 13, an intimate time of preparing His disciples for what was to come.

One needs to understand in approaching this text that the clear purpose of Jesus' discourse was not to explain eschatology. Rather, He wanted to call the saints to prepare themselves for coming events. Obviously, there was a need for a certain amount of educating and informing concerning those events. But the clear sense of the passage is exhortation, not education.

So what was the commonly embraced eschatology of the first-century Jew before Jesus brought new revelation? It was comprised of several elements, the most notable of which were the following.

First, messianic hope. Old Testament Scriptures made clear this prophecy. Isaiah 53 is the most well-known. Psalm 110 is the most commonly quoted psalm in the New Testament due to its prophetic reference to the Promised One as being the Son of God. Isaiah spoke of a branch (4:2; 11:1). The Davidic covenant in 2 Samuel 7:8–16 proclaimed that His kingdom would be a forever kingdom, and Micah 5:2 prophesies His birth in Bethlehem, the City of David.

Second, the day of the Lord. This is the long-awaited cataclysmic destruction of all the world as a judgment from God. Amos 5:16–20 and Isaiah 13:6–16 are two important passages that sought to clarify for those who may have thought this day was going to be a day of rejoicing. Instead, it will be a day of destruction.

Third, the resurrection of the dead. When Jesus talked with Martha about the death of Lazarus, Martha's comment lets us see in a window to the prevailing Jewish eschatology of the day. "I know he will rise again in the resurrection at the last day" (John 11:24). Mark 12:18 indicates that the Sadducees, one of the leading Jewish sects of Jesus' day, did not believe in a resurrection, but Acts 23:8 indicates that the Pharisees, which was by far the more popular of Jewish sects, did hold to this teaching.

Fourth, judgment. Jude 14–15 indicates a prevailing prophecy of judgment. Enoch, the seventh from Adam, prophesied about these men: "See, the Lord is coming with thousands upon thousands of his holy ones to judge everyone, and to convict all the ungodly of all the ungodly acts they have done in the ungodly way, and of all the harsh words ungodly sinners have spoken against him."

A Dialogue That Provoked (Mark 13:1–4)

As he was leaving the temple, one of his disciples said to him, "Look, Teacher! What massive stones! What magnificent buildings!" (v. 1). The building of mention was indeed one made to impress. It was the second Jerusalem temple, the first having been destroyed by Babylon in 586 B.C. This temple constructed under the direction of King Herod the Great took forty-six years to complete. Josephus wrote of this impressive structure: "The wall of the front was adorned with beams, resting upon pillars, that were interwoven into it, and that front was all of polished stone, insomuch that its fineness, to such as had not seen it, was incredible, and to such as had seen it, was greatly amazing" (Antiquities XV, 11:5). The disciples were duly impressed.

"Do you see all these great buildings?" replied Jesus. "Not one stone here will be left on another; every one will be thrown down" (v. 2). Jesus quickly cooled the disciples' excitement by announcing in very strong language that it would all be destroyed. While not reflected in the English, the Greek text reveals the use of the most emphatic form of the negative. Jesus used this form twice in this prophecy to make His pronouncement even more demonstrative.

As Jesus was sitting on the Mount of Olives opposite the temple, Peter, James, John and Andrew asked him privately (v. 3). Having taken a retreat upon the Mount of Olives, Jesus was now alone with four of His closest disciples. They were stimulated by the provocative prophecy made by Jesus (v. 2), and they wanted to follow up for more information. They asked two questions: **"When will these things happen? And what will be the sign that they are all about to be fulfilled?"** (v. 4). There are two underlying assumptions that are present in these questions: (1) Jesus as the Son of God has knowledge of future and end-time events, and (2) such colossal events would certainly be preceded by signs of warning.

A Discourse That Predicted (Mark 13:5–13, 31)

The questions of the disciples reap a most enlightening and thoroughgoing discourse about end-time prophecy (or eschatology). In Mark 13, there are fifteen statements of prophetic prediction provided by Jesus (as indicated by future tense verbs), or twenty-three statements if each statement is counted literally. All but one of them (v. 2) appears in this second section of the chapter. Together they form a litany of prediction. We must remember that this series of prophetic predictions comes in answer to the two questions in verse 4. In other words, these fourteen predictions are the signs that lead up to the big event; they are the indicators that such an event is imminent. The interesting point about this passage is that one of these signs is the visualization of "the Son of Man coming in clouds with great power and glory" (v. 26). The next sign is the gathering of the church: "And he will send his angels and gather his elect from the four winds, from the ends of the earth to the ends of the heavens" (v. 27). Now, many of us have always thought of these events as the "main event," but verse 29 gives us something to think about: "Even so, when you see these things happening, you know that it is near, right at the door." The "it" here appears to be a reference to the previously mentioned events, including the coming of the Son of Man and the gathering of the elect. This would mean that these events point to and lead up to something else, the "main event."

WORDS FROM WESLEY

Mark 13:7

How happy is the Christian's lot,
Whom saved from every anxious thought
No earthly evils move;
In vain the storms of trouble rise,
Come to his city in the skies
He sits secure above.
Tumults and wars serene he sees,
They cannot interrupt his peace,
Which Christ's approach portend,
Which hasten the long wished for day,
When heaven and earth shall flee away
And grace in glory end. (PW, vol. 11, 61)

We would assume that given this long list of predicted events, the last of the events predicted is the main event. So what is the main event? If this logic is followed, it is the total, cataclysmic destruction that is mentioned in verse 31: **Heaven and earth will pass away.** It is prophesying the destruction of the heaven and the earth. As Jesus said in verse 7, **When you hear of wars and rumors of wars, do not be alarmed. Such things must happen, but the end is still to come. The end** here seems to refer to the end of civilization as we know it, meaning that the main event is the total destruction of heaven and earth as well as the ushering in of a new heaven and earth. This is supplemented elsewhere in Scripture as being the predicted order of things (2 Pet. 3:7, 10; Rev. 20–22). Also in 1 Thessalonians 5:2–3, "The day of the Lord will come like a thief in the night . . . destruction will come on them suddenly." The day of the Lord is a common theme in Scripture and typically refers to a day of utter destruction and judgment (see Amos 5:16–20; Isa. 13:6–16; Joel 2:30–31).

This section is concluded by the reassurance that Jesus' **words will never pass away** (Mark 13:31).

WORDS FROM WESLEY
Mark 13:11–12

The Holy Ghost will help you. But do not depend upon any other help. For all the nearest ties will be broken. (ENNT)

A Call to Prepare (Mark 13:32–37)

In this section, Christ turned from predicting the signs to preparing the saints. He included five elements in His call to prepare.

Ignorance of Timing. Obviously, we are not told how much time will pass before these events take place or when they will occur. **No one knows about that day or hour, not even the angels in heaven, nor the Son, but only the Father** (v. 32). His purpose here was not to set our clocks or our calendars, but rather to prepare our hearts.

WORDS FROM WESLEY
Mark 13:32

Of that day—The day of judgment is often in the Scriptures emphatically called *That day. Neither the Son*—Not as man: as man He was no more omniscient than omnipresent. But as God He knows all the circumstances of it. (ENNT)

Importance of Constant Readiness. Jesus had in mind three godly purposes for keeping everyone in ignorance as to the timing:

- Alertness—**Be on guard! Be alert! You do not know when that time will come** (v. 33). God wants us to be alert to Him at all times and for all purposes, not just because of impending judgment.

- Faithfulness—**It's like a man going away: He leaves his house and puts his servants in charge, each with his assigned task, and tells the one at the door to keep watch** (v. 34). God wants His children (servants) to be going about His business, constantly doing His will and fulfilling His purpose. We all have our assigned task, and faithful is the one who does it well.

- Vigil—**Therefore keep watch because you do not know when the owner of the house will come back—whether in the evening, or at midnight, or when the rooster crows, or at dawn. If he comes suddenly, do not let him find you sleeping** (vv. 35–36). This is a call to be spiritually awake at all times. Of course, the life of holiness is one of constant communion and total devotion. A person who lives such a life will not be caught sleeping.

Insight of Stewardship. The best way to prepare for the day of the Lord is not to sit around reading all the end-times books and news articles, watching all the movies, and keeping up on the latest eschatological views. Rather, the Lord has given us work to do as His servants. He has entrusted a responsibility to each of us. To faithfully carry out those duties is the kind of watching He wants of us. But our watching should also be reflected in our character. The best "watchers" are those who, in the words of Paul to Timothy, "watch [their lives] and doctrine closely" (1 Tim. 4:16). Those who walk in holiness with vigilance have no fear in the final day. "Therefore . . . be all the more eager to make your calling and election sure. For if you do these things, you will never fall, and you will receive a rich welcome into the eternal kingdom of our Lord and Savior Jesus Christ" (2 Pet. 1:10–11).

Intensification of Warning. There are seventeen command forms in this chapter. But a closer reading of the original text indicates that the call to watch is intensified as the passage moves into this last section. Three different vocabulary items are used in these six verses to call the saints to *watch*, *be on guard*, *be alert*, or *keep watch*. Of these, two of them are used more than once in these verses. A total of five command forms dominate this final section, and they all serve to call to watching.

The Universality of the Appeal. This passage concludes with a statement indicating the universality of the call to prepare: **What I say to you, I say to everyone** (Mark 13:37). It was not solely for the disciples who asked the question or even the people of Jesus' day and place. This call to prepare and be vigilant at all times is universal; it is for everyone, everywhere, at all times. Let us take this message to heart for our day.

DISCUSSION

Throughout human history, we've always been intrigued with knowing what the future holds. (If we're honest, we'd often like to know what our personal futures hold.) Questions of determinism versus individual choice define most religions, including Christianity and of late even scientific thought. Since Adam and Eve, we have been grappling with the fundamental question of our future: Who is in control of it?

1. Do you have reservations about eschatology, the study of Bible prophecy? If so, what are they? What encouragement, if any, have you received from the study of Bible prophecy?

2. Read Mark 13:1–13. Do you think it is right to look for signs of the end times? Why or why not?

3. How would you define "the day of the Lord"?

4. According to Mark 13:7–8, what is the possibility of lasting world peace in our lifetime? Defend your answer.

5. Why do you agree or disagree that it is helpful to read books about the end times?

6. How does the certainty of the second coming motivate you to lead a holy life?

7. How would you answer a distraught unbeliever who asked, "What is this world coming to?"

PRAYER

Lord, keep us awake and alert, always ready for Your return. Give us the wisdom to dismiss those who claim to know the exact time of Your return. May we fulfill the earthly responsibilities You have given us, while always looking up, ready to meet You in the air.

A DAY THAT CHANGED HISTORY

Mark 14:32–36; 15:25, 33–39; 16:1–7

Jesus' resurrection brings new life!

The doctors delivered the grim news to Jenny's two adult sons. She would not revive from the cancer surgery. It would be only a matter of minutes before she passed away. The prognosis came at noon on Saturday, the day before Easter Sunday. Soon, the rest of the family and the pastor gathered at Jenny's bedside, but she was still faintly breathing long into the night.

Suddenly and unexpectedly, to the doctors' amazement, Jenny awoke at 3:00 a.m. Easter Sunday. "Where am I, and what time is it?" she asked. When the startled family members told her it was 3:00 a.m. Easter morning, Jenny insisted on singing a resurrection hymn. It was an Easter that family and hospital staff members would remember for a long time. This study deepens our love for the One who died and rose again.

COMMENTARY

Jesus spent His last days on earth trying to prepare the disciples for what was to come. What an impossible task! Nothing Jesus said or did could fully ready those disciples for the horror that lay before their good rabbi or the joy that would be theirs at His resurrection.

Jesus had shared a final meal with the Twelve. There He instituted the symbols of the new covenant, a covenant He would usher in through His obedience to His Father's plan. He broke the bread and poured the wine. These were pictures of what He would physically be doing, allowing His body to be broken and His blood to be poured out as the final sacrifice.

As the hour approached, He needed to spend time with the Father in order to be strengthened for what lay ahead. In order to gain the full impact of our victory in Christ, we must travel the entire pathway with Him from Gethsemane through the resurrection. We cannot fully appreciate the empty tomb until we begin to comprehend the suffering that preceded it.

Jesus Prayed in Gethsemane (Mark 14:32–36)

Jesus' arrest and subsequent crucifixion were at hand. Knowing this, He retreated to the **place called Gethsemane** (v. 32), which in Hebrew means "oil press." This was a garden at the Mount of Olives where there were olive trees and olive presses. Jesus had left most of the disciples behind and took only three of His closest friends—**Peter, James and John**—with Him (v. 33). It was a familiar spot to the disciples because it was one of Jesus' favorite places (see Luke 22:39; John 18:2).

Mark tells us that Jesus **began to be deeply distressed and troubled** (Mark 14:33). We can only surmise the fear, anxiety, and confusion in Jesus' heart. Jesus knew the road that was before Him; He knew what He would have to face. And He knew what the Father expected of Him.

"My soul is overwhelmed with sorrow to the point of death," he said (v. 34). As Jesus poured out His heart to these three trusted friends, we can glimpse a tiny portion of what Jesus must have been feeling. Yet these friends were unable to comprehend the full impact of His words.

His instruction to these three was, **"Stay here and keep watch"** (v. 34). Jesus knew His enemies were plotting to arrest Him in the garden. He knew that Judas was already betraying Him, leading the soldiers to this spot where Jesus often went to pray (John 18:2).

Going a little farther from them, Jesus began to pray. He requested that **if possible the hour might pass from him** (Mark 14:35). Some have surmised this meant that Jesus was afraid to go to the cross. But as we look at His prayer, we find a deeper insight into Jesus' words.

WORDS FROM WESLEY
Mark 14:36

I question not but you take the holy Evangelists and Apostles for your pattern, and yield up your whole spirit, soul, and body, a lively, reasonable sacrifice to Him who has an absolute dominion over you by right of creation, preservation, redemption, and sanctification. 'Father, not My will, but Thine be done' was, we know, the prayer of the holy Jesus; and so must it be ours, likewise, otherwise the same mind is not in us that was in Him. But you, my dear brother in Christ, I am persuaded, are already blessed by our Heavenly Father with the inestimable gift of His Holy Spirit. Oh cherish that divine guest within you, and keep the heavenly flame of divine love burning upon your heart, and pray earnestly for His continual abode with you. Never grieve Him, in no wise quench Him, and He will, by degrees, open to you the wonders of His love towards poor, darkened, diseased mortals. (JJW, vol. 8, 301)

He began by praying, *Abba,* **Father** (v. 36). This was a most intimate term and can be translated from the Aramaic as "Daddy." He was not being disrespectful. Rather, He was speaking to the One with whom He had the closest of relationships. He continued, praying, **Take this cup from me** (v. 36; see also 10:38–39). The cup symbolized the wrath of God. Jesus had perfectly followed the Father's plan. He had never experienced separation from God because of sin. He had never experienced God's anger or disapproval. By going to the cross, Jesus would take on himself the full judgment of God for all the sins of the world. Jesus was questioning whether He would be able to stand up to this kind of judgment. He was dreading going into the darkness of separation from God and taking on all the punishment for the sins of the entire world—past, present, and future.

Yet in the midst of His anguish, Jesus still was totally submissive to the Father's plan. He prayed, **"Yet not what I will, but what you will"** (14:36). Throughout Jesus' life on earth, He was totally obedient to God's will. Even in these final desperate moments alone with the Father, He still had that same singleness of mind and heart. May we follow Christ's example in walking according to the Father's plan.

Christ Was Crucified (Mark 15:25, 33–39)

Mark records that it was at the **third hour** when Jesus was led away to be crucified (v. 25), which would have been 9 a.m. Then **at the sixth hour**, about noon, **darkness came over the whole land** and stayed **until the ninth hour** or 3 p.m. (v. 33). No explanation is given. Perhaps Mark wished us to see it as a picture of God's judgment on our sin.

Interestingly, Mark only recorded one of Christ's words from the cross: *"Eloi, Eloi, lama sabachthani?"* (v. 34). It was Jesus' cry through the darkness of God's judgment. It is a cry that reveals His feelings of abandonment: **"My God, my God, why have you forsaken me?"** (v. 34). Jesus had been betrayed by Judas, denied by Peter, and deserted by His disciples, yet He only cried out as the Father turned His face from Him when He bore the sin of the entire world. He cried out as He drank the cup of God's judgment for all of us.

In His final hours, as in His entire life on earth, Jesus was misunderstood and mistreated. People nearby mistakenly thought He was **calling** out to **Elijah** (v. 35), whom the Jews regarded as a deliverer of those in trouble. **One man** tried to offer Him **wine vinegar** (v. 36), which was usually given as a narcotic to help relieve pain. But other skeptics in the crowd didn't even want Him to experience that little bit of comfort.

WORDS FROM WESLEY

Mark 15:34

My God, my God, why hast thou forsaken me—Thereby claiming God as His God; and yet lamenting His Father's withdrawing the tokens of His love, and treating Him as an enemy, while He bare our sins. (ENNT)

Finally, after hours of torture, Jesus died (v. 37). Then **the curtain of the temple was torn in two from top to bottom** (v. 38). This was the curtain that divided the Holy Place from the Holy of Holies—the place where God was said to dwell. Jewish historians tell us that the curtain was thirty feet wide and sixty feet long and as thick as the palm of a person's hand. It was made up of seventy-two squares that were sewn together. It is said that it took three hundred priests to move the curtain, yet Scripture tells us this curtain was **torn in two from top to bottom**. Truly this was the work of a supernatural God! Although Mark did not relate the spiritual significance of the curtain tearing, the writer of Hebrews explained what it meant (Heb. 9:1–14; 10:19–22). It was a sign that the barrier to God had been removed. The curtain was a symbol of the flesh of Christ, which was torn so we might draw near to God through the finished work of the cross.

Many of the eyewitnesses mocked and scorned Christ. But there at the foot of the cross was a centurion who was in charge of the soldiers administering the corporal punishment of Jesus. He had seen many men die by crucifixion, and he observed everything about our Lord's death. Seeing how Christ died, he declared, **"Surely this man was the Son of God!"** (Mark 15:39). Whether or not he realized the impact of his words, we do not know. But he, in fact, recognized the greatness of Christ and spoke absolute truth identifying who Jesus really is—the Son of God.

Jesus Is Risen (Mark 16:1–7)

A group of women had watched Jesus die on the cross (15:40–41). These had been faithful followers of Christ throughout His ministry. They had served Him when He was in Galilee and had come with Him to Jerusalem to do the same.

Even in His death, they still had a desire to serve Jesus. Although His disciples scattered in fear, the women set aside their fearfulness to show one last act of love and devotion. They desired to prepare Jesus' body for burial. There had been no time to do this because of the Sabbath. And **when the Sabbath was over** at 6 p.m. Saturday evening, some of these women gathered and **bought spices . . . to anoint Jesus' body** (16:1). However, it was probably too dark to find their way to the garden tomb, so they waited until after sunrise.

On Sunday morning, they went **to the tomb** (v. 2). Their greatest concern was who was going to roll away the stone from the tomb so they could tend to Jesus' body (v. 3). They had no idea that the tomb had been sealed and a guard had been posted there (Mark 15:46–47).

Upon arriving at the tomb, **they saw that the** large **stone** had already **been rolled away** (16:4). And **as they entered the tomb, they** found what is described as **a young man dressed in a white robe sitting on the right side** (v. 5). Although Mark did not specifically identify him as an angel, the fact that his garb is noted as white helps us understand that this was none other than an angel of God.

Of course the women's first reaction was fear. One commentator explained their response as being dumbfounded. But the angel eased their fear and announced, **"He has risen! He is not**

here. See the place where they laid him" (v. 6). He not only told them the news of Christ's resurrection, but he also drew their attention to the evidence that Jesus' body was gone.

It is significant that angels announced Jesus' birth to the shepherds outside Bethlehem and His resurrection to these faithful women. Both shepherds and women were considered outcasts in the society in which they lived and were unable to testify in court. Yet these are the ones to whom God chose to first announce His message. He gave a voice to the downcast by entrusting them with the gospel message, and He does the same today. It is important that we see that the message of God is sent to those who are ready to receive it, not necessarily those whom society would expect or respect.

The angel's final instructions were to **go** and **tell** Jesus' **disciples and Peter** (v. 7). Peter was specifically mentioned of all the disciples. He had denied Christ three times on the night He was arrested. He probably felt he had failed so badly that he disqualified himself as someone whom God could use. God wanted Peter to know He wasn't through with him. He wanted him to understand that failure isn't final and that God is gracious and merciful to all who repent. Peter needed the added assurance that he was still an instrument in God's hand that could be used for God's purposes.

The angel also told the women to convey the message that Christ was **going ahead** and would meet them in **Galilee** just as He had told the disciples (v. 7). The purpose of meeting them in Galilee is not explained. A large part of Jesus' ministry happened in Galilee. Galilee was far enough away from Jerusalem that the disciples' fears could begin to subside. Jesus had set up His ministry headquarters in Capernaum, which is located in Galilee. It makes sense, then, that He would join His disciples there.

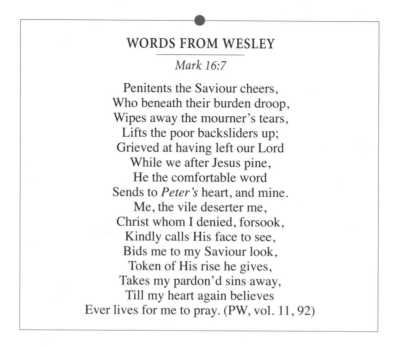

WORDS FROM WESLEY

Mark 16:7

Penitents the Saviour cheers,
Who beneath their burden droop,
Wipes away the mourner's tears,
Lifts the poor backsliders up;
Grieved at having left our Lord
While we after Jesus pine,
He the comfortable word
Sends to *Peter's* heart, and mine.
Me, the vile deserter me,
Christ whom I denied, forsook,
Kindly calls His face to see,
Bids me to my Saviour look,
Token of His rise he gives,
Takes my pardon'd sins away,
Till my heart again believes
Ever lives for me to pray. (PW, vol. 11, 92)

But most important was the fact that this fulfilled what Jesus had told them prior to His death. They would remember He had said that after His resurrection He would meet them in Galilee (Mark 14:28). Christ's words to us are always fulfilled. Both Christ's crucifixion and resurrection are documented historical events. Both were prophesied and fulfilled. Therefore, we should never doubt that His promise to come again in glory will also be fulfilled just as He said.

DISCUSSION

Jesus' death was a triumph, not a tragedy. He accomplished the purpose for which He came to earth, and then He arose from the grave.

1. As you read Mark 14:32–36, what emotions do you believe Jesus experienced at the time?

2. How do you gain a better understanding of Jesus' humanity from reading Mark 14:32–36?

3. What evidence of Jesus' close relationship with God do you find in Jesus' prayer?

4. Have you prayed, "Not what I will, but what you will," when facing a difficult situation? If so, what was the situation?

5. Why did God "forsake" Jesus during the crucifixion?

6. Why is it significant in your life that Jesus gained direct access to God for you?

7. If someone asked how you know Jesus is alive today, what would your answer be?

PRAYER

Lord, give us the ability to empathize with Jesus' suffering, to stand with Him as our friend and brother. Give us the courage not to scatter when persecution comes, but to stand firm to the end.

WORDS FROM WESLEY WORKS CITED

ENNT: *Explanatory Notes upon the New Testament,* by John Wesley, M.A. Fourth American Edition. New York: J. Soule and T. Mason, for the Methodist Episcopal Church in the United States, 1818.

ENOT: Wesley, J. (1765). *Explanatory Notes upon the Old Testament* (Vol. 1–3). Bristol: William Pine.

JCW: Wesley, C. (1849). *The Journal of the Rev. Charles Wesley.* (T. Jackson, Ed.) (Vol. 1–2). London: John Mason.

JJW: *The Journal of the Rev. John Wesley, A.M.* Standard. Edited by Nehemiah Curnock. 8 vols. London: Robert Culley, Charles H. Kelley, 1909–1916.

PW: *The Poetical Works of John and Charles Wesley.* Edited by D. D. G. Osborn. 13 vols. London: Wesleyan-Methodist Conference Office, 1868.

WJW: *The Works of John Wesley.* Third Edition, Complete and Unabridged. 14 vols. London: Wesleyan Methodist Book Room, 1872.

OTHER BOOKS IN THE
WESLEY BIBLE STUDIES SERIES

Now Available in the Wesley Bible Studies Series

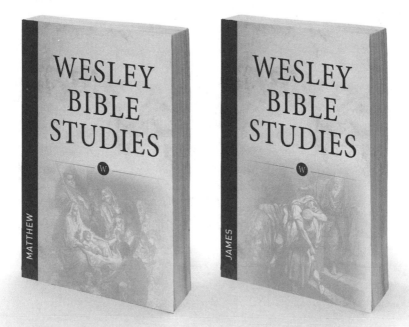

Each book in the Wesley Bible Studies series provides a thoughtful and powerful survey of key Scriptures in one or more biblical books. They combine accessible commentary from contemporary teachers, with relevantly highlighted direct quotes from the complete writings and life experiences of John Wesley, along with the poetry and hymns of his brother Charles. For each study, creative and engaging questions foster deeper fellowship and growth.

Matthew
978-0-89827-862-0
978-0-89827-863-7 (e-book)

James
978-0-89827-840-8
978-0-89827-841-5 (e-book)

wphonline.com
1.800.493.7539